# PRACTICAL NE(
## in 90 MINU⎿ES

For a complete list of Management Books 2000 titles,
visit our website on www.mb2000.com

> The original idea for the 'In Ninety Minutes' series was presented to the publishers by Graham Willmott, author of 'Forget Debt in Ninety Minutes'. Thanks are due to him for suggesting what has become a major series to help business people, entrepreneurs, managers, supervisors and others to greatly improve their personal performance, after just a short period of study.

**Proposed titles in the 'in Ninety Minutes' series are:**

- Forget Debt in Ninety Minutes
- Understand Accounts in Ninety Minutes
- Working Together in Ninety Minutes
- Supply Chain in Ninety Minutes
- Networking in Ninety Minutes
- 25 Management Techniques in Ninety Minutes
- Practical Negotiating in Ninety Minutes
- Find That Job in Ninety Minutes
- Control Credit in Ninety Minutes
- Faster Promotions in Ninety Minutes
- Managing Your Boss in Ninety Minutes
- Better Budgeting in Ninety Minutes
- … other titles may be added

**The series editor is James Alexander**

Submissions of possible titles for this series or for management books in general will be welcome. MB2000 are always keen to discuss possible new works that might be added to their extensive list of books for people who mean business.

# PRACTICAL NEGOTIATING in 90 Minutes

A guide to successful negotiating practice –
a discussion of skills, strategy and tactics –
including a section on team negotiating.
Case Studies and Check Lists are included to
demonstrate negotiating in real situations

## Stephen Morse

2000

Dedicated to David Brown of PMS York

Copyright © Stephen Morse 2005

All rights reserved. No part of this publication may be reproduced, stored in a retrieval system, or transmitted in any form or by any means, electronic, mechanical, photocopying, recording, or otherwise without the prior permission of the publishers.

First published in 2005 by Management Books 2000 Ltd
Forge House, Limes Road
Kemble, Cirencester
Gloucestershire, GL7 6AD, UK
Tel: 0044 (0) 1285 771441
Fax: 0044 (0) 1285 771055
E-mail: mb2000@btconnect.com
Web: www.mb2000.com

Printed and bound in Great Britain by Digital Books Logistics Ltd of Peterborough

This book is sold subject to the condition that it shall not, by way of trade or otherwise, be lent, resold, hired out, or otherwise circulated without the publisher's prior consent in any form of binding or cover other than that in which it is published and without a similar condition including this condition being imposed upon the subsequent purchaser.

British Library Cataloguing in Publication Data is available

ISBN 1-85252-456-1

# Contents

Chapter 1 – Definitions, Situations and Skills      7

Chapter 2 – Preparation      23

Chapter 3 – Psychological Preparation      39

Chapter 4 – Structure and Strategy      64

Chapter 5 – The Influence of Behaviour      92

Chapter 6 – Team Negotiation      108

Chapter 7 – Summing Up      118

# 1

# Definitions, Situations and Skills

This book is about Negotiating. Oh, by the way, did you negotiate with the bookseller when you bought it? Did you suggest to him or her that if he provided you with something extra – a 2 for 1 deal, a next year's Diary, a free ball-point pen – you might be prepared to buy the book, otherwise you'd get it on the Internet, or borrow a friend's copy or go to another shop? After all, perhaps you said, *'It's a book about negotiating – so let's negotiate!'*

But you probably didn't have time or the assistant had no authority to do anything except ring it up on the till, or you had already decided to pay the price for the immediate satisfaction of possessing the book, the cost of the book being worth paying – without argument. What a complicated set of considerations are involved whenever negotiation is possible or likely!

In a recent article in the Times, John Naish describes how he discovered that haggling, bargaining or negotiating could be attempted in a few chain stores (camera shops, for example); independent hi fi shops (*'We have to recognise that we live in the real world and if we don't haggle with someone, then they're going to move on to another shop.'*); bicycle shops – tempting anxious buyers with 10% off and adding variables such as helmets, lights etc. into the bargain; in car showrooms where the 'sticker' price is the 'hoped-for price'.

And he suggests you should haggle with the computer emporia in Tottenham Court Road, and for anything second-hand – jewellery or antiques are often marked up with high margins which may be negotiated down. Naish concludes that you need 'a bit of front and a pleasant manner' to be successful in achieving price discounts and reductions. Indeed, the Office of Fair Trading has produced a leaflet encouraging purchasers to 'be assertive', to 'negotiate on the price you're offered', to 'shop around', 'complain', and to 'remember businesses are competing for your money. If you don't ask, you don't get.' (A small question arises, even before we get involved in more sophisticated negotiating, 'will such aggressive approaches really achieve the results you are seeking?')

Thus the areas where negotiation does or does not take place need to be established early on. There are large number of areas where it is advantageous to negotiate as Naish indicates – and possibly we duck out of many of them. 'We can't be bothered', 'We're too frightened', 'It's not done', 'It puts us in a bad light' are some of the excuses we use to comfort ourselves. These excuses are often validated because the strategies, tactics and skill have not been considered.

*Note: negotiators are both masculine and feminine. Where 'he' and 'his' are stated, please also think 'she' and 'hers'.*

## Negotiable subjects

That's why this book is about those things – strategies, tactics and skills, and why we must start with a list of subjects we can (and should) negotiate about.

- **Buying a house.** And what about leaving the curtains, and not removing all the light- bulbs? and what about an after-sales 'help-desk' for the purchaser?

- **Wages or salaries for a new job.** Or do I hear a hoarse laugh from someone saying: 'negotiate wages?' – and of course it depends on the employment situation, whether your skills (as a shelf-stacker!) are in demand, and how far the potential employer can add inducements such as length of contract or pension.

- **Price.** Perhaps it can be balanced against delivery, payment terms

## Definitions, Situations and Skills

or specification. Is it possible to negotiate to have a simpler version or do you have to have the one with all the unnecessary features you don't really want? 'But just think what else you are acquiring ... the most modern, future-proof product ...!'

- **Payment terms.** Must we pay cash? – how about a cheque? – must I pay immediately? – how about what used to be called 'Hire Purchase' (now probably 'delayed payment', with no interest for the first six months)? – monthly terms? – what about a credit card? – what about a discount for cash?

- **Specification.** 'But can't I have the sun-roof and the quadraphonic radio for the same price?' 'I'm afraid, sir, they only come as standard in the automatic model. It might cost a little more to have the standard gear-shift model fitted with those extras' – and so on ... There is always a standard spec, but individual requirements can often be negotiated – if you try!

- **Industrial relations.** There have been so many high-profile stories of the negotiating of industrial relations that it seems unnecessary to list them. (When you have finished this book, you may be able to pick out the errors made by the negotiators in an industrial relations story!) But, seriously, often an examination of particular cases can provide illustrations of structure, strategy and tactics, and the stages at which the flexibility or pigheadedness of individual negotiators influenced the outcome. Negotiations also take place within organisations and businesses about wages, working hours, supervision and management, pension rights, flexitime, part-time workers, non-union members, health and safety – even travel expenses.

- **Patents, licences and franchise arrangements.** As an inventor, you may establish patent rights and this provides you with rights of ownership provided others may be licensed to use your invention. But neither the licensing rates nor the date when you must allow competitors to use your patent are specified in the patent or copyright regulations. For example, there are three main types of technology patent licensing agreements: (1) Non-exclusive – the organisation granting the license retains the right to license the same technology again to another party; (2) Partially Exclusive – the same technology may be licensed again for a different geographical area or for a different application; (3) Exclusive – the organisation granting the license may not license the same technology again to another party.

Franchising is similarly the licensing of a branded name, process or system – shop types, services like copying (Kall Kwik) or hotels (Holiday Inn) – and what is negotiated is not only the cost of the franchise but often the assistance to be provided by the franchise owner.

- **Copyright**. The situation is similar to patenting. Some written creation – literature, music, pictures – is automatically the copyright of the creator, for up to 70 years after the creator's death. Anyone who wants to use it or copy it must pay a fee. Often the fee is 'negotiated', for example for use of the material in a film or TV programme. We shall see later what that may mean.

- **Block booking of accommodation**. One of the more interesting inventions of the 1960s was the 'package tour' – and the idea that a 'tour operator' would put together a package fitting together a hotel room and a seat in an aeroplane. Of course, tour operators had arranged such things as individual travellers on scheduled airlines in the past, but now large numbers of holiday makers could be accommodated on chartered aircraft – all going to the same destination for the same length of time – a fortnight. This meant that the operator had to negotiate both with the airlines to buy charter capacity and with the hotels to find the right number of rooms for his charter passengers. Very often the tour operator was tempted to charter whole aircraft and book all the rooms in certain hotels. The risks in this have been regularly evident in the bankruptcy of those whose forecasting of the tourist market has been over optimistic. In order to sell cheap holidays, the negotiation both with airlines and hotels has been a key function of managing the cost of holidays.

- **Separation and divorce.** Some of the most painful and difficult negotiations take place when there is a marital break-down leading to separation or divorce. The negotiation has the added dimension of the emotional history of the relationship up to that point – psychological baggage which, at times, can act as an almost insurmountable obstacle to settlement.

- **Antiques and objets d'art.** One of the advantages of the antiques auction is that it can replace the difficult 'haggling' where the value of a piece is a matter of 'how much the buyer wants it' against the 'need for the seller/owner to sell it'. Indeed, all negotiation seems to have this conflict at its heart.

- **Second-hand car sales.** Anyone who has purchased a second-hand car will recognise that very many aspects of negotiation appear in this process. The purchaser may feel (and the seller hopes that he or she will feel) that he or she has a bargain. The seller will have a different aim – which may indeed be simply to sell one more car this week within an acceptable price range (see the first model on the following pages). This is an area where the objective clearly determines the strategy each party should follow. The problem is often that a 'professional' (seller) is faced with an 'amateur'(buyer).

- **Contract terms.** Millions of contracts are signed every day – but whether they are for building a hospital, maintenance of railway track, filling holes in the road, setting up a mortgage, renting a property or a hire-car, owning a credit card, or paying a regular bill by direct debit, and many others – negotiation is not only possible, it is, in my view, mandatory. For one thing, unless you have discussed the contract terms with the other party (TOP), how do you know what's in it? How many of us are really au fait with all the details of the contracts we happily put our names to. We may well think differently (and more profitably) when we have studied this book!

- **Ladies of the night.** I suspect that their services may well be negotiable – but when questioned, those involved (either as purchasers or sellers) are naturally somewhat coy.

## Situations difficult to negotiate

And then there are those areas where no negotiation can take place – or when it is really not worth bothering. When you start to make a list, however, you may find that some areas are in fact worth the effort. To start with, take supermarkets; were you to try to negotiate prices you would find obstacles such as 'we don't need to sell to you' and 'no pressure to buy from him' In other words, the supermarket is saying, *'We have lots of other customers who are willing to buy this product at our price'*, and you are saying *'There are plenty of other supermarkets/outlets where I can purchase this product.'* Or, take the price of an hotel room; some consultants have suggested to hotel chains that they should 'price' their rooms in the same way as low cost airlines now do – advance booking is cheapest, prices go up as the time of reservation diminishes; full price is to be paid by those who must travel at the last minute. But most hotels will only reduce their 'rack rate' when a room is still unfilled late at night. So, in fact, it may be worth while negotiating a lower rate at a point when you judge the hotel is likely to have an empty room if you don't occupy it.

Scheduled airlines try to increase their revenue per flight by offering stand-by fares; theatre managements offer cheap seats at the last minute to those willing to queue in Leicester Square.

But taxis with meters, hire cars, rail tickets and petrol prices, though varied, are not truly negotiable. Which illustrates the point that negotiation can only take place when each party is willing to negotiate.

## Defining negotiation

It is helpful to try to define 'Negotiating' clearly, because people have differing views and approaches. [A friend who teaches Negotiating Skills always demands a discount when booking an hotel room. Very many times he gets it straightaway because the hotel keeper does not realise that my friend is simply opening a 'negotiation'.]

One definition which seems to be neutral is:

> **to confer with one another with a view to compromise or agreement.**

The major difficulty with accepting this definition is that the very idea of compromise makes negotiators seem somehow 'weak.' Often, rather than defining negotiation, writers and lecturers describe it as:

> **'the verbal activity through which agreement is lost or made'**

or

> **'in a successful negotiation, both parties gain, but, more often than not, one party wins more than the other.'**

... but which party decides whether the negotiation is successful? Very often, that is precisely the nub of the problem. Often the process is one which appears to be 'attack' and 'defence' – faced with an unreasonable demand, I am doing my level best to fend it off – as I may lose! *(Next time there is a news story about wages or conditions of work, or about commercial development, look at the ways in which both parties react.)* A member of the Fire Brigade's Union defined Negotiation as 'two parties getting together and agreeing on something...' which would seem to a straightforward approach to a definition. But if you think about it, there are huge gaps in the definition – which parties, how should they get together, what do they hope to agree on, does each party have the same or similar objectives? And sometimes it is the 'getting together' which may be the major stumbling block – and that first bit must be separately agreed.

A more useful 'mantra' is that 'Negotiation is always about future relationships' – indeed the negotiation may well determine the size and shape of future relationships. Think of industrial relations, even drawing up peace treaties which, however painstakingly undertaken, may well sour relationships not just for this year, but for generations!

As a working definition I have found the following to cover most of the aspects of negotiation.

**'Negotiation is the practice of a difficult personal skill which can utilise the power of the face-to-face situation in order to gain maximum advantage where conflict of interests exists.'**

Notice the emphasis on the personal and face-to-face skills which should necessarily be involved, and should be recognised in the planning and preparation stages of negotiating. This includes, of course, such aspects as 'body language', choice of spoken language and emphasis.

Notice also that 'maximum advantage' does not necessarily mean either getting all you want or winning. As in court, if guilty, the criminal's defence barrister's 'maximum advantage' may be only a shorter sentence, when the criminal would much prefer to be found 'not guilty'.

Negotiators must, above all, be realistic.

## Negotiation models

A model is devised to provide a general diagram of what happens, (or should happen) when negotiation takes place. A number of models have been produced by those who have been involved in, or have studied, negotiating. A danger to be avoided is to make a 'model' a rigid guide to a step by step approach, and thus miss the interactive nature of the process. *'If I do this, will she do that'* – *'If she does that, what should be my response?'*

Here are four of the most useful models – though it is important to realise they may not apply to every situation.

**MODEL 'A'** is one which purports to be universal, and suggests that there are four key elements in any negotiation:

a) the needs and objectives of the 'seller' (as defined in the broadest terms)

b) the needs and objectives of the 'buyer' (again broadly defined)

c) the ingredients of the negotiation – what the negotiation is to be about – objectives, variables, concessions, and hoped for outcomes

d) the point of balance.

The model suggests that when the needs of the 'buyer' and those of the 'seller' reach a 'point of balance', the negotiation is concluded. The assumption is that you can assess the needs and 'stance' of the Other Party (TOP) and work out the 'point of balance'. This may well be the case when sellers and buyers have been negotiating with each other for some time. In addition, those devising the model have put forward a systematic method covering the identification of the 'real' as distinct from the 'false' stance of the buyer or supplier, the recognition of the kind of terms on which the contract or outcome will be settled – ('ideal terms', 'realistic terms', and 'fall-back terms') and the different negotiating strategies which may be applied by either party in order to reach a satisfactory outcome – 'the point of balance' of the model. This model can certainly provide the structure of a training course, and like all models, it is by its nature simple – but the psychological make-up of individuals can always upset an expected outcome, as we shall discover in some case histories.

**MODEL 'B'** simplifies the process into the idea that negotiating takes place only where there is overlapping interest, and that both parties should start by trying to establish the range of values where negotiation is important to both. (One of the breakthroughs of Golda Meir when negotiating with the Palestinians was in developing the idea of 'land for peace' – the realisation that her constituents longed for 'peace' and the Palestinians for 'land'. Later attempts at negotiation have tried to resurrect these ideas but have stumbled against other 'non-negotiables' (the late Yasser Arafat, suicide bombers, retaliatory oppression and so on))

If one can set up a range of considerations of Party 'B' (buyer) in one direction, and a range of considerations of Party 'S' (seller) – at some point they will overlap.

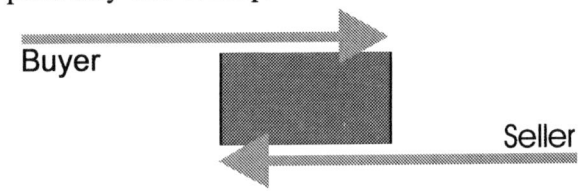

... and that is the area where negotiation should take place.

**MODEL 'C'**, which seems to me to be more practical, is one where the parameters of discussion and expected settlement are described as positions on the map where the following are borrowed from the Model 'A' showing for 'B' Buyer and 'S' Seller:

- **IS = Ideal Settlement**

- **RS = Realistic Settlement**

- **FBP = Fall-Back Position**

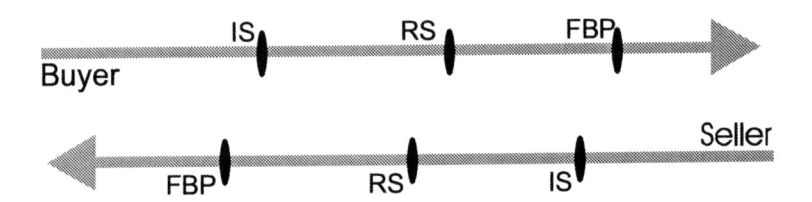

The model suggests that each party should try, initially, to 'suss out' the parameters of the other.

## The Firefighters' dispute began along such lines:

A: 'What about a 40% increase in pay?'

B: 'Ridiculous! Not to be considered!'

A: 'How about £8-50 an hour?'

B: 'What about half now and half later...?
and so on ...

**MODEL 'D'** is also a model which might be used at certain stages in complicated and difficult negotiations in order to suggest possible courses of action. It is usually known as the Levinson *'Balance of Cost'* model.

- A's bargaining power is: the cost to B of disagreement with A's terms, relative to the cost to B of agreement with A's terms

- B's bargaining power is the converse.

Theoretically A or B will take the course of action which will offer the least disadvantage

It is therefore essential to rate the cost of each element likely to be brought into the negotiation by the other party, and the likelihood of that element becoming a cost. The cost of each element can be rated on a scale of 1 − insignificant to 10 = severe − with the likelihood rated as certain = 1 and little chance = 0.1.

Multiply the cost of elements by the likelihood for disagreement and agreement since you are assessing whether the other party will agree or disagree with a particular offer.

> A typical example of this model can be seen in Frederick Forsyth's thriller *'The Negotiator'*. The story is (and I shall not reveal what happens!) that the son of the American President has been kidnapped; a man called Quinn – the 'best negotiator in the world'(!) –

has been brought in, and he uses a ruse to make contact with the kidnappers' spokesperson – Zack.

The elements Quinn has to consider are:
- the boy's freedom
- the hiding place
- the other kidnappers
- the police search
- secrecy
- the ransom.

... all of which may become part of the negotiation and for each of which he must establish the cost. For example Quinn needs to know whether the boy is still alive. So the cost to Zack of agreeing to provide evidence that the boy is alive – which will take him valuable time – is much less than the cost of refusing to provide evidence. Zack asks for $10 million as a ransom. The cost to Quinn of disagreeing is much less than the cost of agreeing; Quinn reckons that this is an opening 'bid'. And so on ...

For every part of a negotiation, as we shall see in the later discussion about preparation, the negotiator needs to ask questions summed up as 'What if ...?

Anther example of the problem which can illustrate this model was described in a letter to *The Times* referring to Yasser Arafat's discussion at Camp David in December 2000.

Dennis Ross, the chief negotiator between the Palestinians and the Israelis at Camp David and Taba in December 2000/January 2001 said that 'on borders, there would be about 5 per cent annexation in the West Bank for the Israelis and a 2 per cent swap,' that 'the Palestinians would have in the West Bank an area that was contiguous' and that it was 'completely untrue' to say there were cantons. Ross also said: 'On Jerusalem, the Arab neighbourhoods of East Jerusalem would become the capital of the Palestinian state.'

Yasser Arafat met President Clinton on January 2 2001. Ross said that 'Arafat said yes, and then added reservations that basically meant he rejected every single one of the things he was supposed to give,' –

such as Israeli sovereignty over the Western Wall, and that Israel should be allowed to fly in Palestinian air space to land at Ben Gurion airport. He presented no counter proposals and walked away from negotiations.

Clearly Arafat had decided at some stage that the cost of 'disagreement' was less than the cost of 'agreement' – and that ending the negotiation was less costly than continuing. He clearly also bore in mind the constituents on whose behalf he was negotiating.

## Background, attitudes and profile of the negotiator

What is evident from these models is that there is no mechanised aspect which a negotiator can apply. They depend for their success not on abstract principles but on the personal attributes of the negotiator, reinforced by some skills training. Some have asked whether there is a born negotiator – and have been told that:

**'The complete negotiator should have a quick mind, but unlimited patience, know how to dissemble without being a liar, inspire trust without trusting others, be modest but assertive, charm others without succumbing to their charm.'**

So the question then arises, how far are such attributes the result of 'nurture' or 'nature'? Nurture, upbringing, social level, education and peer group pressure clearly have a bearing on such questions as

- Do we feel uneasy about making a high/low offer?

- Do we find it essential to have full authority?

- Do we feel that making concessions somehow shows weakness?

- Are these aspects of virility?

- Do we have the courage to be blunt?

And even if the answers to these questions are encouraging, there is still a need for careful training and supervised experience. Too often it is thought (nay, believed!) that a number of human skills come naturally to everyone. ( Betty Macdonald, author of *'The Egg and I'* wrote an autobiographical book whose title came from the immortal phrase in her family 'Anyone can do anything and especially my sister Betty!') Too often, we believe that management, driving a car, sex, making a presentation and negotiation are natural skills which we all possess. Some people may be born with some of these skills. Most people can acquire some of them with training. A few can shine by improving natural ability with skills and training – and perform brilliantly – there is a Dutch proverb which is apposite: 'Skill and assurance are an invincible combination.'

In the list of the requirements of a good negotiator, 'awareness' leads the field. A friend of mine once described this as the ability to look down upon the negotiating scene rather like a TV camera in a helicopter, so as coolly to assess the situation during the course of the negotiation.

When a Minister is due to defend or explain his Department in Parliament, not only is he aware of the major issues affecting his department, but his civil servants have also spent time trying to anticipate what questions will be asked affecting the Department, and producing knowledge-based answers. Unfortunately most negotiators do not have the support of civil servants; which means that it is crucial for the negotiator to have personal, detailed 'knowledge' of the subject matter of the negotiation.

> In the Forsyth book, Quinn spent a great deal of time finding out all about the President's son, and as much intelligence as possible about the background of the potential kidnappers, before he starts negotiating.

This does not mean every detail of, for example, the specification –

just enough to allow an 'educated' discussion with the other party (TOP) about how changes or differences in the spec. can provide TOP with benefits or can concede a change to balance TOP's demand. The negotiator must also know enough so that discussion of detail fits into the structure of the negotiation.

> An announcement in Parliament of a 'billion pound contract for aircraft carriers' was somewhat side-tracked by the MP who said, 'An aircraft carrier is simply a box; it's what goes into the box in the way of weapon systems and the like that's important' The Minister did not take the bait and go down that particular alley at that stage – unwilling to show a lack of detailed knowledge? Such detailed questions or comments can, of course, be used during the negotiation to change the main discussion and relieve or build up pressure.

When a negotiator is being chosen the ability to 'communicate' fluently and confidently is important and may have to be injected. Someone once remarked that in a discussion people were not listening but waiting to speak! Communication skills include not only what to say, but also how to say it, listening carefully to what TOP has said or implied and directing or re-directing one's responses accordingly.

Last but not least, the negotiator must have 'confidence' in his or her own abilities, and a belief in the attainability of his or her objectives. Negotiators who are Buyers need to be reminded that decisions on spending money may be the most important factor. Those who are Sellers must also keep firmly in mind not only the need to sell, but the need to sell profitably – and for many years to come! Confidence thus leads to loyalty to the cause you are promoting or defending.

# Checklist for Chapter 1

- [ ] Did you negotiate with the Bookseller? Who won?

- [ ] Apart from the last one, (or including the last one, if you insist!) which of the fourteen subjects for negotiation have you been involved with?

- [ ] Have you noticed that some subjects are more acceptable than others as susceptible to negotiation?

- [ ] Are fixed prices non-negotiable?

- [ ] How often have you encountered a negotiator who is too low in the organisation to make decisions? (See later discussion of the 'Mandate' and 'Mother Hubbard' Strategies in Chapter 4.)

- [ ] Which of the models do you think might have helped the firefighters' negotiations?

- [ ] Are the attributes of the born negotiator realistic? Do you know one?

- [ ] Which do you think is the most important attribute - awareness, knowledge, confidence or communication skill?

# 2

# Preparation

Preparation is the most important aspect of negotiating – the best prepared negotiator usually gets the best of the bargaining. There are four major features of any preparation:

1) **Objectives**
2) **Assessment of strengths and weaknesses [of both parties]**
3) **Listing variables**
4) **Identifying concessions.**

In the following Case History, the question of preparation appears to be the determining feature in the outcome of the negotiation.

## *Honsang Motors*

### The Buyer Prepares

John Bronowski looked round his new office with satisfaction: a much wider window and a better view than his previous one. Akron, Ohio had, unfortunately not changed and many tall chimneys still filled the atmosphere with the acrid smell of cooking rubber. But his new job, procuring steel pressings for the best selling car – the Honsang SR – was rather daunting. He wasn't looking forward to meeting Mr Dixon today. The main problem, he thought was that Dixon had been very friendly with his predecessor who had now left to go to a job with one of the big rubber companies across town. He went to the filing cabinet, since confidential information was normally not kept on the computer – too easy to hack into, even outside the plant – and picked out the Dixon's file.

Luckily, his predecessor kept his records up-to-date. He found the current contract and noted the date. It was due to end in 3 months time. The price sections of the contract stipulated that the prices would stay firm for a minimum of six months after signing. The only increases after that would be to cover the increased cost of materials – such as steel. John looked further into the file. There seemed to have been no increase at all up to now, nine months on. Then he found a letter from Dixons asking for a 5% increase in the price of the pressings covered under the present contract for its final three months – the reason given was the increase in the cost of steel whose cost had gone up by 10%; the letter pointed out that 50% of Dixon's costs were steel prices.

On the desk in front of him was his own letter to Mr Dixon suggesting a meeting to discuss the next contract, and he had replied quoting prices 5% above the present ones.

|    | Existing Price | New Price |
|----|----------------|-----------|
| X1 | $17.40         | $18.27    |
| Y1 | $15.58         | $16.35    |
| Z1 | $22.58         | $23.70    |

with the price variation provisions exactly as the present contract.

A separate sheet was a copy of the list of quantity forecasts for the three pressings for the next three years which had been sent to Dixons.

|    | Year 1  | Year 2  | Year 3  | Avg Prev.Yrs. |
|----|---------|---------|---------|---------------|
| X1 | 30,000  | 35,000  | 35,000  | 25,000        |
| Y1 | 20,000  | 22,000  | 22,000  | 18.000        |
| Z1 | 12,000  | 15,000  | 15,000  | 10,000        |

## Preparation

After a brief coffee break, John looked at the notes he'd made about the competition for the pressings business. There were two quotes in the file, of which his predecessor had highlighted one – from Acme Pressings of Pittsburg – as being the more interesting. Their prices were quite a bit less than Dixons' new price, and George had made a comparative table.

|    | Dixon's New Price | Acme's Offer | Tooling Cost |
|----|-------------------|--------------|--------------|
| X1 | $18.27            | $17.00       | $48,000      |
| Y1 | $16.35            | $15.40       | $40,000      |
| Z1 | $23.70            | $22.60       | $48,000      |

John thought this quite attractive, except that Acme seemed to be insisting on producing its own tools, rather than using the existing tools (which belonged to Honsang but were at Dixon's plant). Hm, he thought!

Back to the file and the history of the relationship with Dixons over the last 12 years. Gerry Brackett, his predecessor, had been very friendly with Arthur Dixon – who seemed to be the major shareholder in Dixons. According to the file, there didn't seem to have been any problems over the years with their supply: Every so often there was some correspondence about changes to Honsang's production schedules, and praise for Dixon's acceptance of the hiccups caused to the supply chain. There was, however the occasional bleat about Dixon himself being unavailable.

As he studied the file, John became more and more worried. His boss had told him that the secret of successful negotiating was good, solid preparation.

But what should he prepare for? Things looked worse when he looked up the 'Account Status' on his computer and found that Honsang owed Dixons some $240,000 of which two-thirds – $160,000 – was overdue!

And there was a note from the Production Engineering Department warning his predecessor to the dangers of tools being made by any new supplier. This stuff put him in a very weak position.

The other aspect of preparation was trying to assess the Other Party's weaknesses – and he couldn't at this point in time see any. Could he, perhaps, use their vulnerability on price or perhaps the proportion of Dixon's turnover (some 25% he thought) which was dependent on the Honsang business. And who was to say that Dixons might not be taken over by some competitive car maker. Or was that one of his own weaknesses?

He had just finished jotting down a few notes when the buzzer on his desk sounded.

'Yes?' he said. 'Right, send him in.'

Arthur Dixon came in with his hand already outstretched. John rose from behind his desk and came quickly towards him, the chief question in his mind being whether the man now shaking his hand had prepared as well or better than he had.

## Arthur Dixon's work sheet

Arthur Dixon had been negotiating with all his customers for a long time. He reckoned his job was not to 'sell' but to negotiate a satisfactory agreement between himself and his customer. He'd been supplying Honsang for some twelve years and some other customers for five years longer than that. Over those years, he had put together his own Preparation Worksheet – and had used it so often now that it had become automatic. In this case, his preparation had been even more thorough than usual.

- He always started with the fullest possible examination of the Data, checking that Honsang's business was worth about 25% of his (Dixon's) annual $50m turnover. Having to find a replacement would, in to-day's business climate, be very hard. As for the future, the estimates which Honsang (... what was the new man's name? – ah yes, Bronowski) had sent him showed a healthy 16% increase over current business, which would show a fair amount more profit through greater plant utilisation.

- The Price problem was going to be tricky. The increase of 5% for the last three months of the current contract looked reasonable against nine months of price stability. Bit of goodwill could be emphasised there.(He remembered that a consultant who taught Negotiating used to tell him that 'goodwill' never had any value in negotiating – however!)

- But the contract for the next year would have to start at the new level, and take full account of the possible changes in steel prices – and there was some 'catch-up' to make good as the price of steel had already gone up. Bronowski would be bound to try to offset the increase in quantities against the price, suggesting that Dixons would be making more profit.

- Then again, perhaps we could start charging for the refurbishment of the tools.

The next item on his Worksheet was called **Own Strengths**, which he thought were

- (a) the technical expertise which had been acknowledged by Honsang every time they wanted some changes, and

- (b) the fact that Dixons had been supplying parts to Honsang for more than 12 years.

These two might allow him to pitch for more business – after all, the Honsang SR, good though it was, couldn't last for ever. But then he looked at his **Own Weaknesses**. He didn't know enough about the competition, though he believed that Bronowski, as a new boy, would be looking around. He realised he hadn't managed to delegate enough – which meant when problems arose and he wasn't there Honsang got upset. And don't forget, he told himself, competitors might offer a better deal on tooling: refurbishment could only cover the problem for so long, and the wear had begun to show.

Arthur Dixon pulled out his Worksheet Card. Ah, yes, what about Bronowski's Strengths and Weaknesses?

First of all, Honsang might get lower prices from a competitor. Acme are short of business and might try very hard. Then Bronowski could use potential future business on a new project as a carrot for a concession from Dixons. But Bronowski also had some weaknesses.

- Bad payment history – $160,000 overdue cash will put him in a very weak position: though he may also blame it on the overhaul in his Accounts Department.

- Another of his weaknesses might be his lack of background knowledge of the relationship of Dixon to Honsang. But then he could also start with a 'clean sheet' ... (What was that about the worthlessness of 'goodwill'?)

Arthur Dixon wondered vaguely why the next item – **Objective** – was not at the top of the Worksheet. Here the objective was clearly to clinch the contact for the amounts suggested at a target price, 5% above present levels – and to get the same price for the last three months of the current contract. Settlement terms should be firmer – perhaps a penalty of 21% for late payment – a change from the current 'net monthly account'. And the contract terms to cover increases in steel prices more quickly – ? backdated.

More important, he always thought, were **Variables** and **Concessions**. One of his pet arguments with his staff was about Variables. He would say that you have to identify those elements in the negotiation process which can be varied without affecting the underlying value of the contract or the route to the Objective – such things as, he would say, the way the price is calculated (per kilo, per metre, per day, per load).

In the case of Honsang, these would be the pricing of each pressing, the payment terms (so long as we get the money in full!), retrospective rebates or discounts, transport costs, stockholding ('just-in-time' arrangements), cost or otherwise of spares, currency of payment, contract law where foreign sales are concerned, and delivery dates and quantities – all these could be considered as 'Variables' when preparing to negotiate. They allow flexibility and can be a strength for the protagonist.

But his staff would also ask, 'D'you mean that the Variables are always negotiable or are they fixed?'

And he would answer, 'They are brought in when you want to say, 'If I do this, will you do that? Or, if I give you this will you give me that?' You use them if it strengthens your case.'

Arthur Dixon also knew that his Worksheet (or the Index cards he always carried with him) also covered the Concessions, which, if pushed, could be offered on a 'Give or Take' or 'Swap' basis. On his Honsang list, his concessions included 'possible movement on price', 'discount for prompt payment' 'flexible delivery quantities or stockholding'. He expected that Bronowski's list of concessions would include the carrots of more business – a chance to bid for a further range of pressings, increased penalties for late

## Preparation

payment, and, of course, signing the contract this afternoon!

He always insisted to his staff that concessions were the building-blocks of negotiation. They work, he'd say, at the point on his favourite model where each side's Realistic Settlement seemed to overlap.

The final header on his Worksheet was **Strategy** which covered his ideas as to how his objective was to be reached. A couple of strategies in this case he thought might be

- (a) to exploit the competitive situation (with the tooling argument, say) or

- (b) using the payment record ($160,000 overdue)as a 'big stick' – remembering to 'tread softly but carry a big stick.

A strategy he thought he might find difficult to work was the one he had used with Gerry Brackett, namely to emphasise past relationships, and the difficulties and delays of changing suppliers for an on-going product like the Honsang SR. Bronowski, being new, probably wouldn't fall for that.

---

A number of questions now arise, once you have read the case so far. You, the reader, are now at the point where John Bronowski and Arthur Dixon are face to face. In some TV quiz shows the presenter asks, *'What do you think happened next?'* In order to answer that question, you will need to study the case slightly more carefully – and now that you have the case history in front of you and it is very straightforward and realistic – whose preparation was more thorough?

### Bronowski

Let's start with Bronowski. He just looked through his predecessor's file and boned up on the history of the relationship with the supplier, recognising perhaps, that his weakness was lack of knowledge of the past. He had not, however, noted his strengths, such as the fact of the contract he had to award – nor had he recognised his weakness in the delay and uncertainty if he changed suppliers, whether the price of the pressings was lower or not.

## Dixon

Dixon, on the other hand, had painstakingly followed his Worksheet and tried to establish what kind of problems he might face. Bronowski was, perhaps, right to be apprehensive in the face of a practised 'seller', who had managed to maintain his business with Honsang over a period of time – but would Dixon come across as over confident? That danger might arise if, having all the details at his finger-tips, he assumed that his superior knowledge and the history of the relationship would carry the day.

So the questions which are not answered by studying the case so far is, what are Bronowski and Dixon actually like? What sort of people are they? Are they both clever enough to recognise the strengths and weaknesses of the other? Or have they both, before the encounter, formed a fixed view of the other?'

In this case the two protagonists have not necessarily been chosen as expert negotiators. Their 'day-jobs' are quite different. Bronowski is responsible for procurement, for purchasing supplies for the assembly plant to use within a stated budget. Dixon is responsible for ensuring profitable sales of his business output. However in both cases, 'Negotiating' comes with the territory, whether they have high levels of skill or not.

That being the case, would Bronowski, being new in the job, be firm in trying to keep the price down by pointing out the cheaper quotes from Dixon's competitors. and brush aside the relationship Dixon had had with Gerry Brackett? *(You might try putting yourself in the position of Bronowski and asking yourself what you would do – and why.)*

But if Bronowski started along the 'competitive tack', what would Dixon do? He is, remember, a seasoned negotiator, and would certainly realise that Bronowski would be under pressure in his new job to produce results. Would that realisation allow him to offer some concession (*allowing* B to produce results!), and how should he produce such a concession? – an 'if I give you this, will you give me that' approach. Perhaps he could say, 'If I let the present price ride for the rest of the contract, will you be prepared to give us a 5% increase for the new contract – firm for six months and after that negotiable?' *(Now put yourself in Dixon's shoes – do you feel comfortable or belligerent?)*

Dixon might well, recognising his strength, start with a tough line – saying in effect, *'Even if you go to a competitor, you will still owe us $240,000, and the change in supplier will certainly cost you more than the lower cost of the competitor's pressings ...'* To which you, in the role of Bronowski would be tempted to take an equally tough line, saying, perhaps, *'Well, we had thought of extending the contract to two years instead of one ...'*

*(As Bronowski or as Dixon, you now find yourself on a track leading nowhere, and you will as either party need to retreat into the 'variable' or 'concession' area – remembering that the Ultimate Sanction – whatever that might be – always leads to a negative situation for both parties, i.e. everyone loses! And by 'Ultimate Sanction' I mean a breakdown in communication – 'I shall just have to take the next train' ... 'the Intifada' ... a Strike.*

*In the framework of the model, when each side gets to the Fall-Back Position, the main objective must be to continue the Negotiation.)*

Missing from Dixon's Preparation Work Sheet is possibly his assessment of the situation in the light of his favourite model (see page 16 in Chapter 1). If he had filled out the details of the model, he might more clearly have identified what might be termed 'sub-objectives' for a number of different aspects, and realised that he needed to establish for each 'sub-objective' the **Ideal Settlement, Realistic Settlement** and **Fall-Back Position**. This might have helped him to avoid deadlock. For example, in terms of a 'sub-objective' on price, Dixon's Ideal Settlement could be 'more than 5% increase of the next 15 months'. A Realistic Settlement would be '5% for the new contract' and a Fall-back Position, 'no increase in price'.

Also in his preparation he might have created a sort of 'ready-reckoner' of prices, quantities. One of the lessons he would have learnt is never to have to resort to a calculator – it interrupts the flow of the negotiation and may well allow the opponent (the other party TOP) time to think.

*(If you were to have to give advice to Bronowski, what particular aspects would you emphasise. The case demonstrates the need for thorough preparation, so that B. can avoid deadlock.)*

## Preparation worksheet

Now we can look at the basic Preparation Worksheet. Using the Honsang Motors Case Study, my colleague provided this detailed instruction.

- Sound and thorough **preparation** is essential to the success of any negotiation.

- One has to distinguish between the basic knowledge and abilities the negotiator has and the preparation that is specific to a particular negotiation.

- For example, in the Honsang Motors Case, basic knowledge will include product knowledge, market knowledge, financial knowledge and legal knowledge among others. This knowledge will be gathered over a long period of time and will be one of the reasons for the negotiator being given authority to negotiate. (Bronowski in the Honsang Motors Case lacked this sort of experience.)

- Each negotiation, however, requires preparation that is specific to that negotiation. Here time is a vital factor. It is essential that enough time be allocated to preparation for the negotiation. The more important the negotiation the more time needs to be allocated.

- With practice the time needed for a thorough preparation can be shortened considerably. In particular the negotiator needs a plan to aid in the preparation.

- The plan should include the collecting together of thoughts under specific headings such as the following:

## Preparation

1. treatment of data
2. your strengths
3. your weaknesses
4. other party's strengths
5. other party's weaknesses
6. variables
7. objectives
8. concessions
9. strategy.

These form the basis of Dixon's Worksheet. Let's look at them in turn.

### 1. Treatment of Data

All the relevant figures should be collected and analysed in advance of the negotiation. The negotiator should insure that the other party gives all the relevant data before the negotiation.

Try to avoid performing calculations in the course of the negotiation itself, as this is likely to put you under pressure and increase your chance of error.

Data summarised might include: (see example on page 35)

- total projected value of the business to be discussed
- effect on your turnover/profit
- effect on Other Party's turnover/profit
- value of previous business
- value of potential future business
- increase in prices
- cost justification of increases
- competitors' prices
- value of percentage savings/increases
- percentage movements and absolute equivalents (don't rely on TOP to be aware of the relationship between percentages, equivalent fractions, ratios and absolute equivalents. If we go back and look at Honsang Motors, the rationale for the request by Dixons for an increase of 5% is that steel whose cost has increased by a tenth over the last six months is half the total cost of the pressings.)

## Honsang Motors – detailed calculations

Total Value of Business at forecast quantities for years 1, 2 & 3 at new prices, and at both new and old prices for previous year's quantities.

|    | At new prices |              | At old prices |                      |
|----|---------------|--------------|---------------|----------------------|
|    | Year 1        | Years 2 & 3  | Previous Year | Previous Year (o.p.) |
| X1 | $598,100      | $639,450     | $456,750      | $435,000             |
| Y1 | $327,000      | $359,700     | $299,300      | $280,440             |
| Z1 | $284,400      | $355,500     | $237,000      | $225,800             |
| Total | $1,209,500 | $1,354,650   | $993,050      | $ 947,240            |

Increase in turnover at New Prices:

for Previous quantity = 4.8%
for Year 1 quantity = 27.7%
Year 1 to Year 2 = 12.0%

Percentages of $1,209,500

1% = 12,095
2% = 24,190
3% = 36,285
4% = 48,380
5% = 60,475
6% = 72,570
7% = 84,665
8% = 96,760
9% = 108,855

Competition

Year 1 quantities:
X1 @ $570,000

Y1 @ $308,000

Z1 @ $271,200
_____
$1,149,200
Saving $60,000 ..................
Tooling..?????????.............

Price reductions in percentages:

|    | $     | 1%    | 2%    | 3%    | 4%    | 5%    | 6%    | 7%    | 8%    | 9%    | 10%   |
|----|-------|-------|-------|-------|-------|-------|-------|-------|-------|-------|-------|
| X1 | 18,27 | 18.08 | 17.90 | 17.72 | 17.54 | 17.36 | 17.17 | 16.99 | 16.81 | 16.62 | 16.44 |
| Y1 | 16.35 | 16.18 | 16.02 | 15.85 | 15.70 | 15.53 | 15.37 | 15.20 | 15.04 | 14.88 | 14.71 |
| Z1 | 23.70 | 23.46 | 23.32 | 22.99 | 22.75 | 22.51 | 22.28 | 22.04 | 21.80 | 21.56 | 21.33 |

## 2. Your strengths
The successful negotiator always thinks positively. You should therefore identify your own strengths and conduct the negotiation to these strengths. Never underestimate your own position as this leads to the unnecessary giving away of valuable concessions.

Possible strengths might be:

- ↑ competition (when buying)
- ↑ monopoly source (when selling)
- ↑ you might be an existing supplier
- ↑ you have technical expertise
- ↑ there is potential future business
- ↑ personal relationships – (a slightly dangerous strength!).

## 3. Your weaknesses
Identification of your weaknesses enables you to prepare adequate counters if the weaknesses arise in the course of the negotiation. With some forethought weaknesses can even be turned into strengths.

Possible weaknesses might be:

- ↓ business going through a bad patch
- ↓ time
- ↓ late payments
- ↓ competition (when selling)
- ↓ design changes, which can create costs
- ↓ lack of personal relationships.

## 4 & 5. The other party's strengths and weaknesses
Try to put yourself in the shoes of the other party. Identify TOP's strengths and weaknesses, which can often mirror yours. Note the arguments which might be put forward; but your strengths are not necessarily TOP's weaknesses, and vice versa.

## 6. Variables
Assuming that the objective of the negotiation is to reach an agreement where a difference exists, then some movement has to take

place – on both sides. It is therefore necessary to identify those elements of the 'contract' (say) that are subject to variation. Practically anything can be turned into a variable even if previously fixed.

Possible variables:

- price
- payment terms
- retrospective rebates/discounts
- transport
- stockholding ('Just-in-Time' requirement?)
- spares
- currency established (in import/export)
- law of contract – (whose?)
- terms of contract – length of time, revision dates etc.
- delivery (road, rail, air, local agency)

## 7. Objectives

The negotiator should be quite clear about the results he or she is expecting from the negotiation. Results specified in general terms (e.g. price reduction) are objectives. Results laid down on specific, quantified terms (e.g. 10% price reduction) are targets.

Possible objectives in the Honsang Motors Case:

- price reduction — - how much?
- price increase — - how much?
- settlement terms — - how much and when?
- fixed price — - how long?
- delivery — - when?
- terms of contract — - which ones?

## 8. Concessions

Concessions can be the building blocks of the negotiation. Having identified the results that you want out of the negotiation (your objectives) it is necessary to identify what you are willing to concede – or give in exchange (your concessions).

Possible concessions – from either party.

- more business
- movement on price
- longer contract periods
- legal terms (e.g imperfection rate)
- larger delivery quantities
- improved delivery.

Whether buying or selling, the final concession which removes all doubt is agreeing to sign the order!

## 9. Strategies

Possibly the most difficult part of the preparation. The strategy is the means by which the objectives are to be achieved. It may be that alternative strategies have to be prepared and used in some negotiations.

Possible strategies:

- exploiting the competitive situation (for Bronowski)
- emphasising past relationships and the difficulty of changing suppliers (for Dixon)
- using the prospect of more business to reduce the price (for Bronowski)
- taking the price of each product separately and talking it through (for Dixon)

Further discussion of various other strategies is part of Chapter 4.

## Checklist for chapter 2

- [ ] In the Honsang Motors Case, why do you think Bronowski was worried – inexperience, relationship with his predecessor, lack of knowledge, unstructured preparation?

- [ ] Why had Arthur Dixon prepared carefully for the meeting – routine (his worksheet had become automatic), apprehensive of the new man, to-day's business climate, proportion of his own turnover at stake?

- [ ] Have you put yourself in either Bronowski's or Dixon's shoes – or both? who won?

- [ ] Do you always need such detailed preparation? Can you establish the risk of losing?

- [ ] Why are past personal relationships often dangerous to rely on?

- [ ] When you use a worksheet, do you check afterwards on the result?

# 3

# Psychological Preparation

A very important aspect of preparing to negotiate – or preparing to 'go into a negotiation' – as perhaps politicians and trade unions might call it, is the whole area of psychology. What is the Other Party (TOP) like? What idiosyncrasies do they possess? What drives them? For a discussion of the psychological preparation involved, this chapter will outline Transactional Analysis (TA) and Social Styles (or styles of behaviour). Both of these approaches are attempts to describe patterns of behaviour. Knowledge of them may help negotiators to prepare strategies for coping with expected behaviour. But since psychological preparation covers both characteristics and motivations, I also discuss some of the stimuli which can motivate TOP favourably or unfavourably, either from the outside or by personal manipulation.

## Characteristics

Those characteristics which are relevant to negotiators may be summed up as 'the consistent pattern of actions that a person uses when in the presence of other people' – in other words, his or her behaviour. It is in the examination of the pattern of that behaviour that the initial work of David Merrill and Roger Reid in the 1960s now provides a useful paradigm, or a theoretical structure in which to examine behaviours and put them into meaningful pigeon-holes. What Merrill and Reid did, (and all those who have taken this approach further) was to postulate that the basic building blocks of behaviour were **Responsiveness** and **Assertiveness** – which they called a 'Social Style Model'. Their real break-through was to combine assertiveness and responsiveness on a grid where assertiveness was the horizontal axis and responsiveness the vertical one. Given – or collecting – some clues about the typical behaviour patterns of a person, that person could be plotted on the resulting two-dimensional grid.

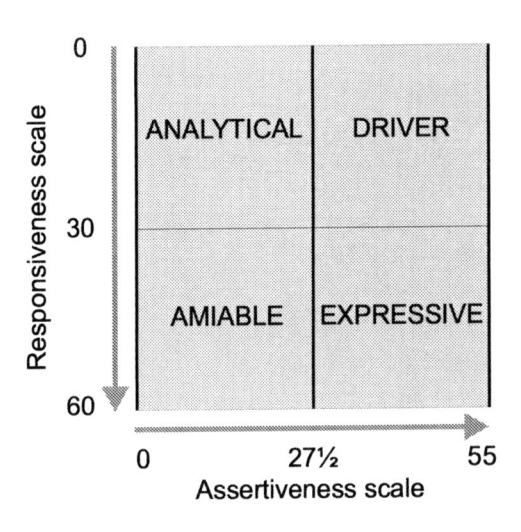

```
                0
                ┌──────────┬──────────┐
Responsiveness  │ANALYTICAL│  DRIVER  │
scale           │          │          │
                │          │          │
            30  ├──────────┼──────────┤
                │          │          │
                │  AMIABLE │EXPRESSIVE│
                │          │          │
            60  └──────────┴──────────┘
                0         27½        55
                    Assertiveness scale
```

The figure shows a vertical *Responsiveness* Scale and a horizontal *Assertiveness* one. The four sections of the figure show four labels. Thus someone who is not very responsive, i.e. at the top of the responsive scale, nor very assertive, i.e. at the left hand end of the assertiveness scale is labelled ANALYTICAL; whereas a DRIVER has a low measure of responsiveness also but is fairly assertive, far to the right on the assertiveness scale. Someone who appears in the lower half of the responsiveness scale, thus high on responsiveness, but low on assertiveness in named AMIABLE. The other section of the is labelled EXPRESSIVE for the person who is very responsive and at the same time assertive.

## Assertiveness and responsiveness

Robert and Dorothy Bolton explain that the Merrill and Reid 'Styles' are shown only in behaviour patterns, and not, as some others have suggested, by attitudes. Nevertheless, some nuances of behaviour are difficult to assign (for example, is a doctor who pushes through a crowd round a sick or injured person with, 'Let me through, I'm a doctor!' being assertive or responsive?). The Boltons suggest using 'the degree to which a person is perceived to be ...' or 'the degree to which a person's behaviours are seen by others to be ...'

It follows, therefore, that if we can assess behaviour patterns, we can be prepared for the outcome of that person's behaviour and can 'negotiate' accordingly. Merrill and Reid's article (in *Business Marketing* 1985) suggest that Sales people can use this form of analysis to improve sales skills. The Boltons in *'Social Style/Management Style'* (Amacom 1984) set out to demonstrate this kind of analysis in improving managerial performance.

**Assertiveness** is described as the degree to which a person's behaviours are seen as being forceful or directive – the degree, for example, to which an opinion is stated with assurance, confidence and force, and the extent to which attempts are made to direct others.

**Responsiveness** might be defined as the extent to which a person's behaviours are emotional or expressive or whose responses are 'emotional'. Emotions might be demonstrated in behaviour.

In order to establish where a person fits in the 'Grid' (see above page 42) one can first create a linear scale as shown, for each attribute. On the horizontal scale of *Assertiveness* one should be able to move from 'Not at all assertive' at the left-hand end to 'Very assertive' at the right. This can be assessed by answering a questionnaire where numbers are attached to each of 11 questions, (say between 5 and zero). The total would be between 0 and 55 on the left to right scale. See page 44.

## Assertiveness scale

Each question describes the extremes (5 = positive) or (0 = negative) of a person's behaviour. Assess on a scale of 5 – 0 each aspect of the behaviour of the selected person. Then enter the total on the assertiveness scale at the bottom of the sheet.

RATING

1. Eye contact is continuous (5) or hardly looks at you (0)   [__]
2. Shows decision-making pressure or lackadaisical   [__]
3. Willing to take risks or risk averse   [__]
4. Decides quickly or takes time to decide   [__]
5. 'Tells' rather than 'asks'   [__]
6. Takes initiative or leaves things to others   [__]
7. Confrontational or hangs back   [__]
8. Expresses strong views or makes tentative requests   [__]
9. Sits upright when giving an opinion or leans back ward.   [__]
10. Speaks quickly and intensely or slowly and deliberately   [__]
11. Moves rapidly or slowly and thoughtfully   [__]

**TOTAL (max 55)**   [____]

## Assertiveness scale

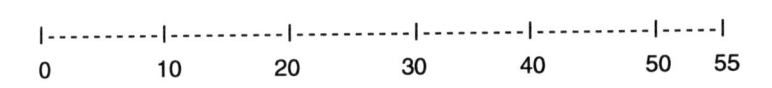

```
|----------|----------|----------|---------|----------|-----|
0         10         20         30        40         50   55
```

A similar scale can be drawn up for responsiveness – this one applying to the vertical axis from 0 at the top (lack of responsiveness) to 60 at the bottom (very responsive).

## Psychological Preparation

### Responsiveness scale

Each question describes the extremes (5 = positive) or (0 = negative) of a person's behaviour. Assess on a scale of 0 – 5 aspects of the behaviour of the selected person. Then enter the total at the bottom of the sheet on the responsiveness scale.

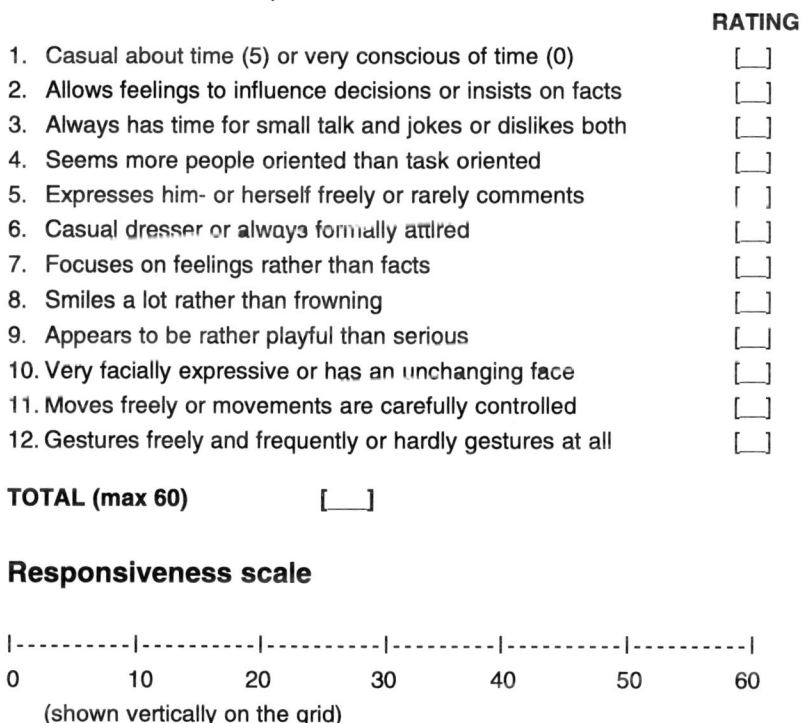

|  | RATING |
|---|---|
| 1. Casual about time (5) or very conscious of time (0) | [__] |
| 2. Allows feelings to influence decisions or insists on facts | [__] |
| 3. Always has time for small talk and jokes or dislikes both | [__] |
| 4. Seems more people oriented than task oriented | [__] |
| 5. Expresses him- or herself freely or rarely comments | [  ] |
| 6. Casual dresser or always formally attired | [__] |
| 7. Focuses on feelings rather than facts | [__] |
| 8. Smiles a lot rather than frowning | [__] |
| 9. Appears to be rather playful than serious | [__] |
| 10. Very facially expressive or has an unchanging face | [__] |
| 11. Moves freely or movements are carefully controlled | [__] |
| 12. Gestures freely and frequently or hardly gestures at all | [__] |

**TOTAL (max 60)**         [__]

### Responsiveness scale

```
|----------|----------|----------|---------|----------|----------|
0         10         20         30        40         50         60
```
(shown vertically on the grid)

Once the figures of each of these scales have been added up and applied to the Grid at page 42 a 'rough label' for the person concerned can be created. In order to check whether this works, try it on someone you know well – or, as a member of a group, apply it to someone the group knows.

You can also find some help (before or after identifying your victim!) by looking at the modified Tracom descriptions of typical behaviours by the different 'inhabitants' of the quadrant (below). The lists cover the major indicators, for example, a Driver shows more assertive behaviours and less responsive behaviours – giving some less predictable clues which may be just the key the negotiator needs.

*(Looking back at Honsang Motors, are there any clues to the behaviour patterns of the two antagonists? Is the office functional? Is Dixon informally dressed or is he neatly and formally dressed?)*

In order to become comfortable with this analytical tool, try it with friends and acquaintances, with colleagues and regular customers or suppliers. For each person, create a behavioural profile and identify where each might fit in the quadrant. When using the questionnaires on pages 44 and 45, don't give middling assessments – tend towards extremes.

And don't forget to apply it to yourself!

## DRIVER

|ANALYTICAL|DRIVER|
|---|---|
|AMIABLE|EXPRESSIVE|

**More assertive behaviours**

- Moves quickly
- Demonstrates task-focused energy
- Sits or stands upright or leans forward when making a point
- 'Tell oriented'
- May speak more rapidly
- Vocal intensity – may sound forceful without speaking loudly (some Drivers also speak loudly!)
- Intense eye contact when making a point
- Expresses facts and opinions more strongly
- Phrasing is direct, down-to-earth.
- More risk oriented

- Decides more quickly
- Exerts more pressure for decisions

## Less responsive behaviours

- Less expression in face
- More controlled body movements
- Limited variety of gestures
- Little expression in voice
- Very task oriented, pragmatic, results oriented
- Fact oriented (versus feeling and opinion oriented) but needs far fewer facts than Analyticals
- Disciplined about time
- Appears more serious
- Not apt to tell stories, jokes
- Often prefers working alone or directing others
- Interactions tend to be brief, sometimes abrupt

## Other, less predictable clues

- Office apt to be functional and may be spartanly decorated
- Clothing is functional, neat, action oriented, rarely splashy
- Leisure time may be spent actively; often likes competition
- Prefers brief reading material, perhaps short mystery stories or technical articles.

## Typical characteristics

- Independent, candid, decisive, pragmatic, efficient

## ANALYTICAL

### Less assertive behaviours

- Slower-paced walk and gestures
- Usually talks and gestures less than more assertive styles
- 'Ask oriented' – even when making statements or giving directions
- Speaks with quieter voice
- Slower, more hesitant in speech, and careful in choosing words
- May stop in mid-sentence, then begin a new sentence that makes more sense to the speaker, though the listener may get lost or frustrated
- Expresses ideas more tentatively and qualifies them
- Tends to lean backwards when talking
- Less risk oriented; emphasises quality – do it right so you don't have to do it over; careful research – focused on details; examining many options
- Decides more slowly
- Exerts less pressure for decisions.

### Less responsive behaviours

- Restricted body movement; gestures are fewer, smaller, and stiffer than other styles
- Little facial expression
- Little variation in voice; may tend toward monotone.
- More task oriented
- More fact oriented
- Disciplined about time

- Appears to be more serious
- Appears detached from feelings
- Not apt to tell anecdotes, jokes
- May like to work alone

**Other, less predictable clues**

- Office decor may be tasteful, conventional, neat, and formal
- Style of dress may be more conservative, proper, and not so colourful
- May prefer solitary leisure activities; may spend more time reading; of all styles tends to spend most time doing technical reading

**Typical characteristics**
- Logical, thorough, serious, systematic, prudent

## AMIABLE

**Less assertive behaviours**

- Slower-paced walk and gestures
- May not talk much, especially in a group
- Soft voice; speaks less intensely
- Speaks less rapidly
- Tends to lean backwards even when making a point
- Invites others to express opinions
- Tends to be quiet in meetings; may express ideas after others have spoken
- Ideas presented may be a combination of the ideas of others who have spoken; may offer a compromise or synthesis

- Expresses proposals more tentatively
- Less risk oriented; conversation may focus on guarantees
- Decides more slowly
- Exerts less pressure for decision

## More responsive behaviours

- People oriented; team oriented, and more apt to remember personal data about others, send birthday cards or gifts, and be concerned how people will respond or be affected by a proposed change
- Prefers one-to-one interactions or small groups to solitary activities or larger groups
- More feeling oriented; responds to feelings of others (though tries to avoid conflict and anger)
- Friendly facial expression and eye contact
- Relaxed posture
- Flowing, non-dramatic, non-aggressive gestures
- Moderate range of inflexion
- More flexible about time.

## Other, less predictable clues

- Office space may be informal and homely, with family pictures and so on
- Dresses informally, but in tasteful conformity
- Prefers to spend leisure time with people; emphasis in reading tends toward biographies, fiction and inspirational literature.

## Typical characteristics

- Supportive, cooperative, diplomatic, patient, loyal.

# EXPRESSIVE

### More assertive behaviours

- Fast-paced motions and gestures
- Usually brimming with energy
- Tends to speak louder than other styles
- Speaks more rapidly, with few hesitations
- Sits or stands upright or leans forward when trying to persuade
- 'Tell oriented'
- Expresses opinions more strongly
- More risk oriented
- Decides more quickly
- Exerts more pressure for decisions
- Initiates projects
- Dislikes routine

### More responsive behaviours

- More large, free-flowing gestures than other styles
- More eye contact and facial expression
- Greatest range of vocal inflexion, tone and volume
- Flowing, more dramatic use of language
- Playful and fun-loving
- More apt to tell jokes and stories than other styles
- May wander from the topic
- Least disciplined about time
- People oriented – the most gregarious of the styles
- Feeling oriented – the most disclosing of the styles
- Fluctuating moods
- Has strong opinions, often based largely on intuition

## Other, less predictable clues

- Office may be open, colourful, bold and disorganised ; may have trophies in office or inspirational posters on wall
- Flamboyant and colourful styles of dress
- Prefers spending leisure time with people partying, competing and so on
- Least reading oriented of the styles; may like inspirational literature

## Typical characteristics

- Outgoing, enthusiastic, persuasive, fun loving, spontaneous

Merrill and Reid in their initial research pointed out that each behavioural style presented both strengths and weaknesses . But what they first did was to list the attractive against the unattractive features of each style, as shown in the chart opposite.

The Boltons suggest that many of the demonstrated behaviours become weaknesses when the person is put under stress – as is often the case when negotiating. And they give examples as follows for each of the main Styles when under stress (perhaps 'stressed out' is the current phrase!)

- An Analytical who is 'precise' becomes 'nit-picking' or if 'systematic' becomes 'inflexible'.

- An Amiable who is 'supportive' becomes 'conforming'; if 'easy going' becomes 'permissive'.

- An Expressive who is 'enthusiastic' becomes 'overbearing'; if 'imaginative' becomes 'unrealistic'.

- A Driver who is 'determined' becomes 'domineering'; if 'objective' becomes 'unfeeling'.

|  | Attractive | Unattractive |
|---|---|---|
| **DRIVERS** | Strong-willed | Pushy |
|  | Independent | Severe |
|  | Practical | Tough |
|  | Decisive | Dominating |
|  | Efficient | Harsh |
| **ANALYTICAL** | Industrious | Critical |
|  | Persistent | Indecisive |
|  | Serious | Exacting |
|  | Orderly | Moralistic |
| **AMIABLE** | Supporting | Conforming |
|  | Respectful | Unsure |
|  | Willing | Pliable |
|  | Dependable | Dependent |
|  | Agreeable | Awkward |
| **EXPRESSIVE** | Ambitious | Manipulative |
|  | Stimulating | Excitable |
|  | Enthusiastic | Undisciplined |
|  | Dramatic | Reacting |
|  | Friendly | Egotistical |

## Responding to patterns of behaviour

The value of this form of analysis lies in the fact that the dominant 'style feature' of a person's behaviour is the one in which he or she feels comfortable. If one must negotiate with a person, then it is necessary first to assess the features of that person's behaviour – and then to modify one's own style to fit in with the behavioural pattern which TOP feels comfortable with.

## Social styles – further action points

|  | DRIVER | EXPRESSIVE | AMIABLE | ANALYTICAL |
|---|---|---|---|---|
| 1. Back-up style | Autocratic | Attacking | Acquiescing | Avoiding |
| 2. Personal values measured by: | Results | Applause | Attention | Activity |
| 3. For growth needs to: | Listen | Check | Initiate | Decide |
| 4. Let them save: | Time | Effort | Relationships | Face |
| 5. Needs climate that: | Allows to build own structure | Inspires to their goals | Suggests | Provides details |
| 6. Take time to be: | Efficient | Stimulating | Agreeable | Accurate |
| 7. Support their: | Conclusions and Actions | Dreams and Intuition | Relationships and Feelings | Principles and Thinking |
| 8. Give benefits that answer: | WHAT | WHO | WHY | HOW |
| 9. For decisions give them: | Options and Probability | Testimony and Incentives | Guarantees and Assurances | Evidence and Service |
| 10. Speciality: | Control | Social | Supportive | Technical |

On one occasion I was trying to sell a series of training courses to a Human Resources Manager, and had made an appointment to see him. It so happened that I was shown into his office when he was out for a few minutes. I noticed that his office was very tidy. The files on his desk were lined up. His jacket was hung on a coat hanger at the side of a cupboard. I concluded that the 'Analytical' behavioural pattern was the one with which he felt comfortable, that it was unlikely he would make a decision immediately, but would demand to see the whole project outlined in detail. By the time he came back, I had firmly decided that I would only present him with the project and try to establish with him a date when he might make a decision. There was no 'chit-chat'. He immediately started to talk about dates and costs and

## Psychological Preparation

potential trainees – making it clear that he would need to consider the detailed proposal which I had put carefully in line with his other files on his desk! Four days later he agreed with my proposal!

I discuss behaviour modification in more detail in the chapter on Strategy – here we are concerned with Psychological Preparation – and preparing to confront the behaviour of the Other Party.

Verax International Ltd have developed and refined earlier Merrill and Reid diagrams by labelling the two axes PACE (assertiveness) and CONTENT (responsiveness or alternatively emotiveness). They suggest that the vertical axis has at the zero responsiveness point the **task**, and at the maximum responsiveness point **people**. Such concepts are also discussed in research into leadership and the balance a leader has to strike between the task and people.

Verax go further and put forward suggestions as to how to interact with those who demonstrate different behaviours. Even though your own behavioural style is, you believe, antipathetic to that of the Other Party you need to modify or adapt your style to fit TOP (the Boltons call this Style **Flex**). Very many procurement managers or Purchasing Officers show the sort of behaviour that Verax call *'Processor'* (analytical) – neither very responsive nor very assertive. In order to win over a Processor you should observe the following.

- Be on time.
- Be fairly formal in dress and appearance.
- Begin by being systematic and business-like.
- Talk about facts and figures.
- Allow time for him/her to consider facts.
- Don't rush TOP into a decision.
- Agree timetables, review dates, contract provisions.
- Send a post-session report in writing.

You maybe up against a *Controller* (driver) who has little time for 'chit-chat' and will be concerned about getting things agreed and as quickly as possible. Therefore your approach to a Driver should be based on the following tips.

53

- Be prompt.
- Don't try to engage in small talk.
- Lay out your arguments systematically.
- Be specific, clear and to the point.
- Give TOP straightforward options to make a decision.
- Make clear what results will follow.
- Use time efficiently – particularly his time.
- Recognise the 'end' point and depart.
- Be careful to ensure you are not browbeaten.

But what about what Verax call the *Supporter* (Merrill and Reid call the *amiable*), what kind of behaviour will fit him or her? Perhaps the following – as a starting point?

- Indicate there is no rush (*Yes, I would like coffee*).
- Small talk, chit-chat often welcomed by the Amiable.
- Communicate patiently, with questions.
- Ask for feed-back to demonstrate understanding – particularly of implications.
- Agree mutual goals and interests.
- Demonstrate minimum risk.
- Don't make promises you can't keep.
- Invite opinions and listen (see questionnaire on page 93).
- Maintain ongoing contact.

And finally if faced with *Expressors* (Verax) or *Expressives* (Merrill), suitable behaviour patterns would recognise the need to let such styles/persons 'have their head'.

- Be sociable: avoid being dogmatic.
- Small talk and jokes are okay in moderation.
- Focus on the 'Big Picture'.
- Tap into the energy of TOP.
- Create a balance between 'going all the way' with them, and keeping them on track.
- Remember to listen (see above).
- Don't try to compete.

## Transactional Analysis

At the same time as Merrill and Reid were codifying behaviour patterns as a way of improving performance in relation to selling and managing, Dr Eric Berne presented what he called 'Transactional Analysis – a New and Effective method of Group Therapy'. It is Thomas A Harris in his book *'I'm OK – You're OK'* that it is presented as a teaching and learning device. (Since Negotiating is always a transaction between persons, I have included a study of the Harris approach to the subject)

Its basis, crudely stated, is that in any transaction, we behave either as Parent, Child or Adult (note behaviour under the spotlight again) – often demonstrated by what we say and how we say it. A simple example demonstrates the basics of the idea:

| | |
|---|---|
| Small Boy: | 'Can I have an ice-cream, dad?' (Child) |
| Father: | 'No, you can't!' (Parent) |
| Small Boy: | 'Why not?' (Child) |
| Father: | 'Because I say so!' (Parent) |
| Small Boy: | 'Mu-u-u-m!' (Child) |
| Mother: | 'Darling, it's nearly lunch time and you wouldn't want to miss burger and chips through being too full of ice-cream, would you?' (Adult) |

It is suggested that the 'Child' is acting as a result of a 'seeing, hearing and feeling' body of data which the 'little person', having no vocabulary during the most critical of early experiences retains as 'feelings'. The Parent operates from a record of all the 'admonitions, rules and laws' that the child heard from parents and saw in their living. It is described as 'a permanent recording which a person cannot erase, and is available for replay throughout life'. These compulsions, quirks and eccentricities result from the experiences of the three-year old and upwards, but in the creation of the Adult, adult data accumulates as a result of the child's ability to find out for itself what is different about life from the 'taught concept' of life in his Parent and the 'felt concept' of life in his Child.

The following diagram puts the differences between the three aspects neatly.

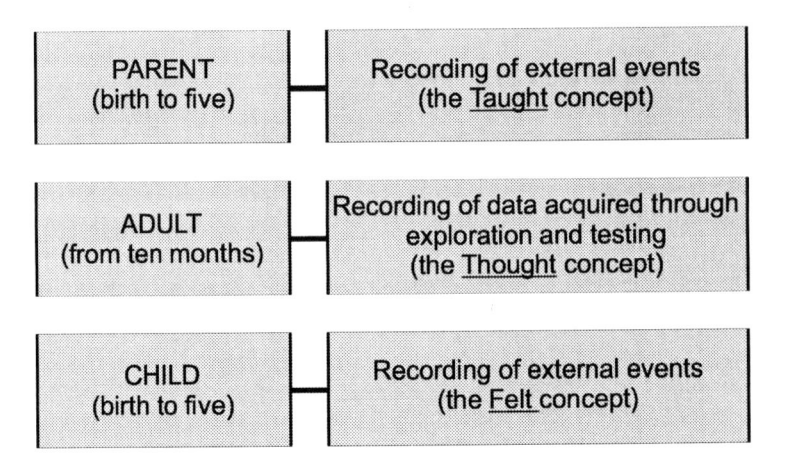

| PARENT (birth to five) | Recording of external events (the <u>Taught</u> concept) |
|---|---|
| ADULT (from ten months) | Recording of data acquired through exploration and testing (the <u>Thought</u> concept) |
| CHILD (birth to five) | Recording of external events (the <u>Felt</u> concept) |

Anecdotes which recognise the transaction between two people, each of whom will choose (wittingly or unwittingly) one of the states shown, can also show where crossed transactions take place.

Harris, in *'I'm OK – You're OK'*, gives an example of what he calls a Crossed Transaction:

Husband asks, 'Dear, where are my cuff-links? *(Adult seeking information)* Wife's reply might be *Adult* as,' In your top left dressing table drawer' or 'I haven't seen them, but I'll help you look.'
However, if 'Dear' has had a 'bad hair day' she might bellow, 'Where you left them!' – having made the response into a *Parent responding to a Child.*

The trick in negotiating is to recognise the Parent or Child in the Other Party and bring the transaction back to Adult. Tying Transactional Analysis and Social Styles together, one can postulate the following – an Amiable (Supporter) might put a request thus, *'Can you really and truly not manage to reduce the price the teeniest bit?'* Being anxious to please, Amiable is reverting to Child. The temptation in that instance is to respond a Parent, *'Of course not.*

*Don't be ridiculous!'* when an Adult response might be, *'I understand, but what can you offer me to balance a concession on the price?'*

## Characteristics summarised

So the process of psychological preparation needs to establish not only the level of Assertiveness and Responsiveness in TOP so as to be able to use the appropriate response – but also to have in the negotiator's armoury the ability to recognise and counter Parent, Child and Adult where necessary. For it is often in a negotiating session when a party is under pressure that what Merrill calls the 'primary back-up style' appears. For example, we all know of the assertive *Driver* who becomes 'autocratic', 'domineering' even; the *Analytical* (or Processor) who becomes 'avoiding' – indeed refuses to make a decision without consultation (for the Mandate Strategy, see Chapter 4.); the *Amiable* (what Verax call the Supporter) who, under stress, becomes 'acquiescent' – agrees to anything, but suffers from a 'mind-change' quite soon; and last but not least, the *Expressive* (Expressor) who may start attacking, flailing wildly in all directions – overacting.

These demand suitable behaviours, ones which advance the chances of you – the negotiator – achieving your objectives. Such behaviours and the preparation for their use probably requires practice beforehand. A training film based on Lidstone's book *'Negotiating Profitable Sales'* is in two parts: the first shows a pre-negotiation rehearsal, in which the expected behaviours of the other Party [TOP], are illustrated and the counter behaviours are discussed and practised; the second part (there are in fact two separate films) is the story of the actual negotiation with a buyer – and demonstrates where the practised behaviours and negotiation strategies can and cannot be used in a 'real' situation. (I am not aware of a training film called 'Negotiating Profitable Purchases')

## Identifying motivations

Of course we don't know whether the Other Party had a row with his wife or whether his children were particularly obstreperous, his subordinate has just done something right, his boss has decided to postpone his promotion – what other good or bad day TOP is having.

Nevertheless, it is possible, thanks to a number of industrial psychologists and researchers, to identify a number of 'triggers' – perhaps to divide them into 'General Motivators', which are probably not controllable by the negotiator, but nevertheless affect the other party – and specific 'persuaders' which may well be operated by the negotiator within the framework of the negotiation.

Abram Maslow's Pyramid is a long established picture of the gradual sophistication of a person's needs, starting at the base of the pyramid with Survival – a physiological need, then the need for Security, a need for safety – possibly the comfort of a daily routine of habitation, eating, travelling etc.

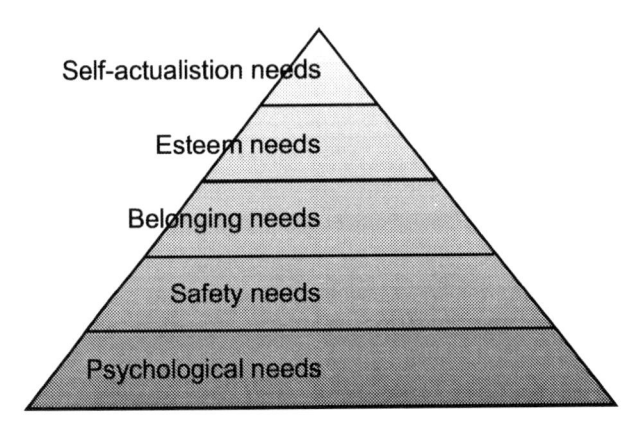

*Maslow's 'Hierarchy of Human Need'*

Then Maslow picks out a Social need, that for love and affection (dogs are more affectionate than cats!) Next to the top of the pyramid is placed Ego – described as the need for esteem – what, I suppose, nowadays would be better described as 'respect'. But at the top of the

## Psychological Preparation

pyramid he places what he called 'Self-actualisation'. It is sometimes translated as self-fulfilment: better, perhaps, the need of most human beings to be themselves – not the son or daughter of parents, not the product of some educational system (a Cambridge graduate) but a person in her or his own right. In passing it is noted, by Maslow, that not everyone reaches the top of the pyramid – but the need remains there!

Maclellan, on the other hand simplifies the business person's need to three: achievement, affection and power – which he sees more as drives than needs. It is possible, I suppose, that taking these drives as a kind of shorthand can be valuable when you are facing the other party in a negotiation. But one can also see that if TOP is not comfortable in the negotiating 'area' – the place is too cold or too hot, too much sun through the window, a long time before lunch – Maslow's Pyramid will start to show its value. For example, if physiologically, TOP is uncomfortable, how about his security? how safe in his job? what are the consequences of error? what about the children's education in their present schools? If TOP is relaxed about survival and security, how about affection or the social atmosphere? at the office, at the pub? at home? Or what about the level of esteem among his/her peers? Very difficult to judge these things. Even more difficult is TOP's level of self-actualisation or self-fulfilment. And these needs are totally out of our control. TOP can do very little about them in the short term – we can do nothing.

Bear in mind also one of Maslow's more profound statements – that each need, or level of needs, has to be fulfilled before the next one up starts to bite. Until a person is comfortable physiologically and feels safe, the need for belonging barely starts – and so on.

The main point is to recognise in the process of preparation that aspects of TOP's character and motivations need to be addressed.

And beyond what we have outlined as *needs*, it is worthwhile to examine what industrial psychologists have discovered as *drives*. In relation to purchasing, they are shown as the overriding, possibly emotional or possibly intellectual or possibly inherited approaches to purchasing/buying – very often one half of the negotiation process. The list describes the major drives behind most purchase decisions, so that if you are a sales person and you are trying to negotiate with a buying person (Purchasing Manager, Procurement Strategy Manager, IT manager etc.) the list may be helpful. The symptoms can usually be attached to a philosopher.

Let's start with the basics.

**Alfred Marshall**, the great economist, could be the one who named 'economic man', whose every purchasing decision is driven by economic considerations – in particular, price *(and, in fact, may not heed Ruskin's warning that 'Someone can always make a product a little worse and sell it a little cheaper, and those who depend on price alone are this man's lawful prey – as quoted on plaques at the Frigidair plant in the USA and at a textile finishing works at Como in Italy)* In times long past, the Consumer Association was guilty of assessing 'Best Buys' on price and efficiency alone and ignoring good design, current fashion, appearance, maintenance costs and the like – clearly heavily influenced by the thinking of Alfred Marshall.

The second philosopher is **Ivan Pavlov** and the concept of 'rewarded learning' (Pavlov's dogs). If one is satisfied with the performance of a product, one will continue to purchase it regardless of competitive offerings – and this goes for everything from cornflakes to cars and computers – and tends to lap over also to Brands. There is a story of a successful car salesman who, before trying to attract a customer's interest in a new car, discussed with the customer at length the strong and weak points of his existing car – so as to understand how strong his 'rewarded learning' might be.

But it is the third philosopher, **Sigmund Freud**, who illustrates the subconscious, fantasy world favoured by many advertisers which is most difficult to identify – the world of Walter Mitty, perhaps. Does the buyer see himself as carried shoulder-high by his comrades when he manages to reduce the asking price by 21%? or herself escorted to the Tour D'Argent restaurant in Paris by a covey of young men for obtaining a retrospective rebate? or are the other party's feet planted firmly on the ground and unlikely to be tempted by 'flights of fancy'?

**Thorstein Veblen** postulated the idea that the actions of individuals were far more influenced by social pressure than was generally understood – often described in a phrase such as 'keeping up with the Jones'. The social group to which one belongs exerts pressures either overtly or sub-consciously on the public actions of the members of that group.

A neat illustration of this idea appeared in Vance Packard's *'Hidden Persuaders' (In the early 1950s an official of the National Shoe Manufacturer's Association declared that 'US men are simply not buying enough shoes' Psychologists concluded that men were held back by a fear of seeming conspicuous in their dress. But the depth merchandiser reasoned that their attitude could be overwhelmed by the increasing desire of men to make a good impression on their peer group ...)*

But we do not need 50-year old examples of this phenomenon. Anyone who watches the unloading of children at a private school will notice within six months the development of a certain sameness in the type of cars used by parents – last year it was a Volvo Estate, then a Mercedes and now a People Mover! Or in terrace houses, a follow-my-leader effect of outside painting – not the same colour, simply the fact of doing it or having it done. And what about football fans – and team shirts?- for the kids?

And finally a word for **Thomas Hobbes**, a seventeenth century philosopher who put forward the idea that one of the major drives of people was the requirement of loyalty to the organisation to which they belong: such loyalty might be expected to override every other drive. An illustration could be members of political parties – an overriding loyalty shaping their actions. (Hobbes didn't put it exactly like that – he wrote that 'in order for the sovereign state to function, we are forced to establish a social contract in which we surrender our rights of 'self-interest' to an absolute ruler, whose commands are the law.')

These are 'drives' – i.e. the tendency of human beings to behave in a certain manner, based, as Hobbes might have put it, on 'enlightened self-interest'. But what about Persuaders – those tools which the negotiator can use in order to push TOP into a 'better' position. In the next panel, I have listed the main ones.

## Persuaders

| POSITIVE | NEGATIVE | |
|---|---|---|
| Force | Threats | |
| Conscience | Fear: | |
| Hunger:<br>- physical<br>- sexual | - physical<br>- mental<br>- of the future | PERSONAL |
| Affection | Boredom | |
| Benefits | Inertia | |
| Pride | Exhaustion | |
| Duty | | |
| Opportunity | | |

| | | |
|---|---|---|
| Status enhancement | What others may think | |
| Group pressure | Fear of: - poverty<br>- disgrace<br>- dismissal<br>- old age | SOCIAL |
| Need for power | | |
| Money | | |

As can be seen, the Persuaders have been divided into four categories. **Positive**, that is those persuaders which persuade the recipient to do something (for example, you use force normally so as to get someone to do something they are otherwise unwilling to do; similarly emotions such as pride or duty may cause the recipient to do something). For these are all emotions or feelings which the

## Psychological Preparation

negotiator can call on to push TOP towards a course of action which the negotiator finds more helpful. The parallel group are those with **Negative** connotations, whose effect may well be to stop someone from doing something (For example, fear or exhaustion can push people towards stopping doing something which they might otherwise attempt – *'if I do not arrange this contract to-day, my boss will come down on me like a ton of bricks'*. Threats are the most obvious negative persuaders.

I have also divided the Persuaders into **Social** and **Personal** – the former are those which operate on a social level, affecting social standing, group pressure and the like, and what others may think and the negative fear, if a particular action or decision is taken the result may be disgrace or dismissal.

Awareness of all these aspects needs to be part of the psychological preparation before the Negotiator meets the other party. Unless there is a sound appreciation of the effects of Drives and Persuaders on TOP it is difficult to go further and discuss the sort of strategies which the Negotiator may be able to use.

## Checklist for chapter 3

☐ **Try creating a grid of characteristics and motivation.**

☐ **Assess your colleagues on the lines of pages 44 and 45.**

☐ **Which persuaders do you feel confident with?**

☐ **What other situations would be helpful in assessing behaviour patterns?**

# 4

# Structure and Strategy

Before considering what kind of strategy might be suitable and whether the structure of the negotiation can be altered in any way, it is useful to ask four questions.

## Is it a negotiation situation?

If you are going into a sandwich shop to buy a sandwich for lunch, the answer to the question would be 'No'. So, simple purchases of standard priced goods are rarely negotiating situations. Nor, probably, is the use of a service. If you are travelling on a train or a bus, you either pay the fare asked or you don't travel. Even on the so-called 'low-cost airlines', what is on offer is at the discretion of the airline. If you are in the produce market at 4pm on a Saturday, you may well be able to get strawberries at bargain prices – the nearest you would get to a negotiation. So, the answer to the first question depends on whether the vendor's prices or conditions are flexible and whether the purchaser finds it worthwhile to obtain some concession. The fact that the vendor is offering discounts to the purchaser for, say, paying by direct debit or booking tickets in advance on the Internet – does not mean that negotiation is either worthwhile or possible.

## Are you a 'buyer' or a 'seller'?

Obviously the strategies used by the purchaser – someone who needs or wants a product or service – will be different from those used by the provider. Similarly the constraints on each will differ. The 'buyer' will always be faced with the twin problems of obtaining the product or service which will satisfy his requirements and not paying too much for it – thus not pushing the 'seller' too far so that he or she withdraws the offer – or 'stalks off in a huff!' The 'seller', similarly, is faced with the need to persuade the purchaser to agree to the conditions of the purchase – and the conditions must give a minimum level of returns for the 'seller'. So he or she must not push the 'buyer' into the arms of a competitor.

## Are the participants (you and the other party) authorised to negotiate?

The basis of successful negotiation is the authority of the parties to 'give and take' – to reduce prices, to change delivery conditions, to alter dates, to offer or accept other variables. A typical strategy operated by some time-share sales people, and some of those who sell kitchens and bathrooms or 'home improvements' (double glazing) is called the Mandate Strategy. This is a strategy where the initial sales person is authorised to reduce the initially quoted price by a certain amount so as to tempt the potential customer. Beyond that point he or she may not go without bringing in 'my manager' (usually the Area Manager, the Regional Manager or the Sales and Marketing Manager) whose authority stretches to some further concessions or 'plus points'. Usually the sales person has judged that the purchaser only requires one small extra concession to agree to the contract or sale. Such a strategy is designed to give the purchaser a psychological boost to think that his or her purchase demands the intervention of a Senior Manager.

## How long should the negotiation last?

This may well depend, of course, on the subject of the negotiation. In the Italacom Case (see below) the supplier was anxious to extend an existing contract, already running for five years, for a further five years, in order to pre-empt the possibility of the user choosing a competitor. The negotiation was spread over three years. So the length of the negotiation will usually depend, for the 'buyer' on the urgency of the need for the product or service, and, for the 'seller', as in the Honsang Motors case, to keep his business afloat. It may also depend on the layers of authority involved. In many domestic decisions the negotiation may be prolonged by 'I'll have to ask my husband/wife' – a situation avoided by some home sales people who will not start negotiating until the both husband and wife are present

## *The Italacom Case – a classic of negotiating*

Italacom Oil is a large multinational oil company (basically Italian in origin) which produces as one of its industrial chemicals Vinyl Chloride Monomer (VCM) which becomes the main raw material for the manufacture of PVC. One of Italacom's European customers is Polvercol (a company in Yugoslavia) whose main business is the manufacture of PVC in its various forms for different uses, whose relationship with Italacom is illustrated by the existence of a 130 km pipeline to carry VCM from the port of Trieste to Polvercol's plant in Zagreb.

**In Year 1 of the case**, the market for PVC is buoyant and Italacom and Polvercol negotiate a contract which will run the five years from Year 2 to the end of Year 6.

For this contract, Italacom's local sales people have based their negotiation strategy on four aspects:

- a past long-term relationship with Polvercol
- an on-going high level of service
- a guarantee in a world-wide shortage of VCM
- a lack of genuine competition to Italacom.

All of which justified the high price Italacom demanded for the supply of VCM.

## Structure and Strategy

**At the beginning of Year 3**, three things happened.

- The market for PVC seemed to be so buoyant that the Board of Italacom in Turin suggested going into PVC manufacture itself – thus competing with its customers!

- The East European Sales team became worried that Polvercol might be tempted to go to another supplier – thus leaving a gap in their customer base! They therefore decided to try to get Polvercol to extend the existing contract past the end of Year 6.

- And at this point (early in Year 3) a new Procurement Manager called Mr H joined Polvercol.

Mr H appears to use two strengths which he has – plenty of time (the existing contract still has three years to run), and his 'offtake' would be very difficult for Italacom to replace. He appears to use these two strengths in two strategies.

- First, he makes a strong demand for some movement favourable to Polvercol (e.g. price, delivery, length of contract), always backed up with very cogent reasons ...

- then he allows plenty of time for the Italacom sales people to consider it by being unavailable to discuss it!

The following is a timetable of events.

| | |
|---|---|
| Year 3 March | Mr H requests a price reduction of 200 lire per litre |
| Year 3 May | After a meeting, Italacom agrees to a reduction of 85 lire per litre |
| Year 3 May | Later, Italacom suggest a 5-year extension to the contract beyond the end of Year 6. Mr H, responds by insisting on only a 2-year extension to avoid being caught in a long-term drop in the price of VCM |

| | |
|---|---|
| Year 3 August | A 3-year extension is agreed. |
| Year 3 Sept | Italacom, still anxious to sign the contract, suggest increasing minimum quantities each year of the contract. Mr H will think about it but is cautious. |
| Year 3 Oct | Mr H agrees an increase of 40% in Italacom's minima, providing there are no changes for 'underlift' (not taking the required quantity within the year). |
| Year 3 Dec | Mr H indicates just a couple of small points to clear up, and then the contract can be signed. The accuracy of the meters at the Italacom end of the pipeline is suspect. New ones should be installed at Italacom's expense at the Polvercol plant end. |
| Year 4 Jan | New meters agreed – but now two other small points are brought up. A couple of clauses should be added, according to Mr H – a 'favoured nation' clause and a 'meeting competition' clause (in effect, 'best prices which must be as low as competitors are offering') |
| Year 4 March | With the new clauses, the contract will be signed by Polvercol provided Italacom allows them to re-sell any surplus quantities of VCM. |
| Year 4 April | Contract signed. |

Looking at the contract Italacom have now signed, from the point-of view of Italacom, they believe they have successfully 'haggled 'a reduction in each of the demands Polvercol has made. In effect, however, they have been outmanoeuvred on each request – the result of not realising that Polvercol's strategy has been triumphantly successful. Each request has been 'unreasonable' – but Polvercol has on each occasion won a concession from Italacom which Italacom were not expecting and had no answer to. Italacom simply did not recognise Mr H's strategy, even after the first climb-downs, and had not prepared any strategy of their own, except to give way as little as possible. They were taken in by the repeated assertion by Mr H that he really

was anxious to sign the contract – and did so after 3 years!
© Stephen Morse 2003

---

As will also be seen in the Italacom case, time was used as a pressure weapon. Having made a demand, the user's representative, Mr H, would be unavailable for several months. The case is also an illustration of the simplest form of strategy – for example, make an unreasonable demand for a price reduction, then wait patiently and be prepared to have TOP agree to, say, half of the demand, which was what the user was expecting anyway.

## Structural essentials

Because this is not a handbook – to be carried around and retrieved from a back pocket when required, or stored on a Palm Pilot or laptop – the discussion of structure and strategy is not limited, as in many books, to a collection of tips, long lists of dos and don'ts which assume that the user of such lists either has them in his head or can apply them instantly to the situation which arises. What I have done is to pick out different situations and point out the sort of structure and strategy which might be, or has been, used.

Using the Italacom Case as a basis, the first essential of the structure must be the **location**. Italacom never seemed to manage to pin Mr H down to a particular location, and for a given length of time. Part of the difficulty must have been that in the locations where the two sides met, contact with decision makers higher up in the organisations was difficult. Perhaps in to-day's world of mobile phones, video conferencing, e mail, text messages and other aids, it might be possible to overcome some of the problems of distance. It is, however, noticeable that for the great political problems in the world, personal contact – whether in Camp David, Oslo or Aqaba – seems an essential in allowing participants to negotiate in a neutral setting.

In humbler circumstances, there are clearly advantages to either party in the location where the negotiation is to be held. Buyers may even prefer to negotiate on supplier's premises. Traditionally, sales people have been itinerant.

One I met many years ago on the Cape Verde Islands in mid-Atlantic who was representing a German manufacturer of all shapes and sizes of knives was on an itinerary which was due to take him to Portuguese Guinea, Angola and Mozambique. It is unlikely that any of his customers would think of going to Hamburg to negotiate their requirements with him.

But look back at Honsang Motors again. Would Bronowski have learnt anything to his advantage by going to Dixon's plant? Would he have realised that Dixon was short of work, and so he, Bronowski, would have had more leverage in keeping the price down, and stretching payment conditions. But Dixon being in Bronowski's office was not, in fact, overawed by the place. He had been there before; he was familiar with the office outlook, the other staff, the level of productivity; he could recognise that Honsang needed his pressings – and would be unwilling to change suppliers at this time.

The Italacom Case is altogether different. It discusses precisely what happened, but not where. The Head Office of Italacom was Turin, and the Polvercol plant was in Zagreb. One supposes that the Italacom sales people went to see Mr H in Zagreb, but if possible they might try to invite him to meet them in pleasanter, nearer places such as Trieste or Venice, and he might counter with Opatija or Rijeka (formerly Fiume) as being more comfortable – and not only with the language. I feel that Mr H would almost certainly force the Italacom sales people to come to him rather than his travelling to Italian cities – particularly as he was intending to make fresh demands at each meeting. Mr H would obviously bear the location very much in mind. The Italians were probably unaware of its importance.

And once decided upon, the location needs other considerations – reachability, by air, by train by car, traffic problems, parking problems and so on.

After location, the second essential has to do with the **participants** in the negotiation. One-to-one meeting is the simplest set-up. But there are often others involved on both sides. If more than one person, then one needs to be sure that everyone involved (on either side) is aware of the objectives and strategy. If the main negotiator has a specialist alongside him or her to help out – with technical details, for instance – 'off the cuff' remarks by specialists should be avoided whenever they are offering a judgement rather than factual information. The details of team negotiation are discussed further in a later chapter (see the Elto and Fabriko Case in Chapter 6) since, when a team is involved, it is most important that each member is clear as to his or her role.

The third essential in the structure is to try to agree with TOP about **timings** – breaks for coffee, lunch or how many days might be involved. It could be that you wish to ensure that breaks or interruptions are in your hands – but then TOP may well feel the same way. *(In the film 'Negotiating Profitable Sales' by Video Arts, our hero creates a pause for thought by supposedly making a telephone call to his Finance Department to ask about a possible change in delivery arrangements. In fact his call is to his boss to play for time. His boss plays along with the conversation and our hero straightens out his thoughts.)* Allowing oneself time to catch up with what has so far occurred and assessing the change in the negotiation stances of oneself and the other party needs what I described in Chapter 1 as 'the ability to look down upon the negotiating scene rather like a TV camera in a helicopter.'

## Structural outline

The outline, while remaining broadly the same, will, in the end, depend on the objectives of both 'buyer' and 'seller', 'manager' and 'worker', 'government' and 'rebel'. It seems that there are examples of negotiations, industrial, personal and political taking place all the time. To use some which might be current during the writing of this book and whose success or failure is at this moment unknown would be a 'temptation too far'. But it is likely that any negotiation, industrial or political, past or current will be able to be divided up into the following stages:

## Opening the negotiation

First, the 'Opening' – the process of trying to assess the other party's total package, and the parameters within which he or she is prepared to negotiate – a most important process, to be undertaken in all circumstances, in order to avoid being caught out by a surprise demand halfway through. *(With the benefit of hindsight the Italacom sales people made no attempt to establish at the beginning the whole of the Polvercol package. As a result they were simply dragged along, one item at a time, and had to fall back on haggling over each. They were thus unable to set one concession off against another – for example agreeing to a drop in the price if the minimum quantity would be raised, or agreeing to an extension of the contract if Polvercol accepted a fixed price for the whole period.)*

Once you have assessed what the other party may be prepared to concede, what the other party is like and what their objectives might be – and if a negotiation is to take place, for it seems unlikely, to say the least, that the status quo will remain unchanged – you can begin to set the outlines of a strategy.

One writer suggests there are two possible underlying strategies the choice of which will determine the attitude of the parties throughout. These are a strategy which leads **'towards agreement'** or one which leads to **'our advantage'** (some writers prefer the jargon of 'Win/Win' or 'Win/Lose' strategies, which I find too unsubtle and facile to describe most negotiation situations). There has been in recent years much heart-searching over the influence in educational establishments of promoting or trying to neutralise the effects of competition. There is still a belief, especially in America, that anyone who doesn't go all out to win at any cost is a 'wimp' or worse. Suggesting therefore that one can choose a negotiation strategy leading **'towards agreement'** can be anathema to some. Nevertheless it is my belief that there are situations when neither side wishes to come out the winner, situations where each party is satisfied with the outcome, situations when the process of negotiation is tinged by the encouragement to co-operation, to stimulate warmth and friendliness rather than pugnacity and antagonism.

If, however, the choice is to develop a strategy **'to our advantage'**, then one will probably be involved with the application of pressure. Pressure can be applied in many ways. (Look back to Chapter 3 and the list of 'Persuaders' as a starting point for decisions about strategies 'to our advantage'.)

Buyers can use hints or threats – they can hint at the existence of competitive tenders, or threaten to take the business to a different supplier. (In passing, it is worth noting that Local Authorities when contracting out some construction or repair work use the written or implied threat that the contractor will not receive future contracts unless the work is satisfactory. Unless the work is supervised while in process or immediately after conclusion, the threat is toothless – largely because the contract also gives a payment date without conditions of satisfactory completion – and the numbers of contractors is so small and the costs of supervision so great that the threats are meaningless.)

A Procurement manager in the Far East was faced with the problem of a monopoly supplier who seemed to be charging very high prices for a raw material whose production he controlled. If you are the only country in the world possessing quantities of this raw material, the temptation to charge a high price is almost irresistible. The strategy chosen by the Procurement Manager was to send a piece to a world-wide journal which covered these kinds of raw materials to the effect 'that there was a strong rumour that a new source of this material had been found in a country on a different continent and would probably come onto the market within about two years.' Without waiting for confirmation of the truth or otherwise of the journalistic speculation, the monopolist dropped his price by 25%.

Threats can also be useful in the areas of delivery and service – 'unless you can deliver within a specified time,' – 'unless we can rely on spares being available for so many years' ...

For the party offering (the sales side of the negotiation), a strategy using positive *persuaders* at the opening of the process can often prove successful. Such persuaders as using the benefits to the other party of agreeing to the offer, 'enhancement of status' by being the unique possessor of the product or user of the service, and, of course monetary inducements (providing company executives with Air Miles when flying on company business was, at one time, a favourite inducement, and for doctors, almost unlimited samples, often unconnected with the pharmaceutical discussed!).

Many advisers suggest that there are golden rules for the opening of a negotiation, namely that the opening should be positive rather than hesitant, and that you should start with the highest defensible bid or the lowest defensible offer – depending on whether you are 'buying' or 'selling' – defensible because otherwise you may not be thought by the other party to be serious. *(Note: In the Italacom Case, the sales people for Italacom opened by merely suggesting that it might be a good idea to negotiate an extension of the contract. Mr H's response was to ask for a price reduction.)*

## Making bids

The second stage is clearly that of 'Making Bids'. But before responding, be sure you understand what the other party is saying – and try to gauge his or her approach – towards agreement or to his or her advantage. Try to avoid being led into the trap of 'justification' of your bid (such as 'because we need to make a profit'). Clarification, on the other hand, is usually acceptable – explaining the bid in other words or terms – either strengthening or softening the original statement depending on the first reaction of TOP. Check each item and avoid speculation on opinions or motives – 'you are just saying that because you think that ... or because your company is wedded to ... a particular set of ideas.'

Your opponent may have extreme views about unrelated topics. Do not engage in discussions about them..

## Assessing advantage

The third stage of the structure can be entitled 'Assessing Advantage.' Here the Levinson model approach is relevant (see Chapter 1 page

17). Just as you will tend to take a course of action which will offer the least disadvantage, you will therefore follow the terms where agreement costs you less than disagreement – and so, you suppose, will the other party. So this stage is aimed at trying to balance the cost of disagreeing against the cost of agreeing. This often means that, as negotiator, you must have an alternative if you are going to disagree – and a follow-up if you agree. For the first, you must offer something as an alternative to their offer/bid: *'We cannot agree with your price – but how about the cost of spares or improving delivery.'* Suppose a Purchasing Manager's strategy is to suggest to a sales person that a competitor has offered a better deal (unspecified) and that he or she should offer a more attractive price. The sales person has to work out whether refusing to offer a better deal will cost more than accepting a reduction in the price.

*The problem demonstrated in the Italacom case was that Italacom sales people seemed always to be caught unprepared and had no strategy to cope with Mr H's demands except to try to reduce the impact in the hope that bending here and there would bring the prospect of the wished-for contract nearer. Mr H realised that the cost to Italacom of losing Polvercol as a customer would be far greater than the cost of agreeing to his successive demands.*

So, 'assessing advantage' means trying to identify and quantify not only what TOP will not accept, but also having an inkling of TOP's absolutely 'must-have' needs as with Italacom – and perhaps taking a view of the possible settlement area – using Models A, B and C from Chapter 1 – and putting the models' theory into practice.

The major findings of a Harvard Study of Negotiating Techniques by Fisher and Ury gives considerable weight to the importance of 'separating the people from the problem'. We have already (in Chapter 3) expanded on the need for preparation on the 'people' aspect. The Harvard Study, recognising the importance of the 'human factors' in any negotiation, discusses three aspects of 'separating the people from the problem'. Fisher and Ury state flatly, *'understanding the other party's thinking is not simply a useful activity that will help solve your problem. Their thinking **is** the problem.'* To try to deal with the situation, they recommend four or five 'tips' which are somewhat reminiscent of the advice of every psychiatrist, mediator or counsellor – and are easier said than done.

It is, however, valuable to take the research study findings seriously and try to anticipate and disentangle the people from the problem. It there is a problem to be negotiated – and if you are negotiating about a disagreement over price or delivery or rights and duties – then each side will almost certainly have a different view of the problem. It may well be helpful then to try to put yourself in the shoes of the other party, express empathy, understand where TOP is coming from. And if you have a problem it certainly doesn't help to blame the other party for it. Because each side perceives the problem differently, it may well help to discuss each other's perceptions. (My view, however, is that Americans are much happier 'baring their souls' than the inhabitants of other parts of the world) It could help things along, though, to give TOP a stake in the outcome and help with the 'face-saving' problem.('Saving face' is one of the more powerful drives among those in power or with high reputations to protect. So-called minor peccadilloes such as dishonesty, gullibility and mistakes can never be admitted by politicians or journalists for example, even though these are among the most common human traits.)

### Emotions

One of the key points of the research study was the recognition of the emotions which may be aroused during the course of a negotiation, and suggests that both parties should recognise and take account of each other's emotions. When groups are negotiating, this becomes even more important: one of the members of one group may find it very frustrating that his or her ideas or proposals have not been taken seriously – and may begin to explode, quietly at first and then noisily. Things get worse when neither side takes any notice.

Fisher and Ury suggest two possible solutions: one is not to bottle up your emotions ('It's my party! I shall cry if want to!'), explain to the other party what a particular line makes you feel; or if you think they are wrong, say what is happening to you rather then saying they are wrong. (Mind you, a grandfather saying he is very hurt by his six-year old grandson's insult falls on rather stony ground. The insult was meant to hurt, after all; demonstrating that the grandfather is hurt merely shows that the shaft has gone home.)

There are, in many group negotiations, circumstances when there is a need to make an insult strike home – to demonstrate lack of knowledge or experience: 'Of course you wouldn't remember...' or 'I don't suppose you would know, would you ...' can appear innocuous, or very hurtful to the victim, depending on 'skin thickness'. There is also the suggestion that you should allow TOP to let off steam. (This might be an interesting suggestion for call-centre staff, who bridle at the merest hint that the complainant is cross, when surely their whole job is aimed at providing a cushion for the Company concerned). So, although we may be tempted to sit back with a superior smile as our opponent lets off steam, we should try to treat it seriously.

## Cultural differences

There may also be a simple problem in trying to communicate with TOP. This hardly occurs between persons who have met several times before, but meeting for the first time can bring problems. These can be categorised first as misunderstanding – there may be cultural differences as between people of different nationality or upbringing, language difficulties even if a translator is involved and idiomatic phrases are used – the joke about a computer translating 'out of sight, out of mind' as 'blind idiot' illustrates the point that we tend to use idioms and sayings all the time in relaxed conversation. (There is saying in Dutch whose literal translation is 'a strange duck in a hole in the ice' – meaning someone who is out of place or even a 'cuckoo in the nest' – which demonstrates there are local idioms and sayings in all languages whose literal translation may not make any sense.)

A problem can also arise when TOP is playing to his or her constituents – the 'powers behind you'. One can notice this when the negotiation takes place or is reported in public – political discussions or trade union disagreements – 'See how strongly I am standing up for your rights', is the sub-text beneath many public pronouncements. The chances of a meeting between negotiators breaking up at 3 o'clock in the morning without acrimony seem to me to be slim. Misunderstandings increase with increasing exhaustion.

But TOP may not actually hear what you have to say. Fran Lebowitz remarked that 'the opposite of talking is not listening: it's waiting to speak'. So Fisher and Ury lay down four rules:

- listen actively
- speak to be understood
- speak about yourself and your feelings
- speak for a purpose.

(At the end of this chapter is a questionnaire on 'How Good a Listener Are You,' where you should honestly tick the answer which applies to you. Attached is a score sheet and comments on the level of your listening. Try looking more carefully at the right answers.)

The fourth aspect of the structure comes after the assessment of advantage. How far have we got? Are we progressing satisfactorily? The following case, 'KOK Submersible', has some interesting points about the structure of a negotiation.

## KOK Submersible Case

KOK are the maintenance branch of a Japanese telephone and cable company – responsible for the maintenance of telephone cables throughout the Japanese islands and other cables outwards from Japan to the Asian mainland and across the Pacific. Their main tools for undertaking their function are cableships and submarines. They are currently trying to obtain a robot-operated 'Submersible' which can be used for shallow water maintenance, up to 750 metres in depth. KOK have already discussed with Undersea Inc. of San Francisco aspects of the proposed submersible, and agreement has been reached on the specification – both parties are content. The commercial aspects of the purchase contract have yet to be agreed.

Mr Tamaka, procurement manager of KOK, looks out of the window of his office on the 15th floor of the KOK building in Osaka towards the busy harbour area.

*Structure and Strategy*

He is waiting for Fred Walbach from Undersea Inc to arrive for discussions on the submersible purchase. Since the cost quoted is $5.2 million (¥650 million), some hard bargaining over not only the price but also the other variables will need to be undertaken. This is Walbach's first personal visit. Contact by e-mail set up the technical discussions.

Mr Tamaka has put together a Preparation Worksheet, starting with the data – all that he knows and needs to take into account in dealing with Undersea Inc.(UI).

## A. Data

- Undersea Inc. from San Francisco has a turnover of $28 million (¥3,500 million) per annum. The price quoted is $5.2 million. (¥650 million).
- Competitor prices are ¥625 m.($5 m) and ¥640 m. ($5.1 m)
- Delivery needed: 12 months     Quoted:   A.16 months
                                                        B. 17 months
                                                        UI. 14 Months
- All offers technically acceptable

## B. Our strengths

- To Undersea Inc., this order represents some 20% of their annual turnover – it would be very difficult for them to find another customer quickly.
- We can possibly order four more subs over the next five years.
- They know us to be a financially reliable and strong business.

## C. Our weaknesses

- We need delivery within twelve months, otherwise our maintenance and replacement of cables programme will suffer.
- We would like to postpone payment till after delivery, but have very little leverage to press for this.
- We may have difficulties in getting a two year guarantee.

## D. Variables

- Liquidated damages (progressive payment for missed delivery dates)
- Payment terms
- Guarantees
- Spares, need for and costs
- Currency of payment – Yen or dollar? exchange rate

## E. Objectives

- To get the UI submersible within 12 months – paying a bit more if necessary.
- To get guarantees and spares on our terms

## F. Concessions

- Possible concession against their payment terms, since we would like 100% payment after delivery

| UI payment terms | KOK offer |
| --- | --- |
| 30% with order | 30% after 30% completion |
| 30% after 6 months | 30% after 60% completion |
| 30% after 12 months | 30% after delivery |
| 10% prior to delivery | 10% retained for 6 months |

- Delayed delivery terms of 2% per week might be reduced if guarantees of 2 years can be offered.
- Other things being equal, could afford the spares cost of ¥60 million ($500K)

Mr Tamaka was a little worried. He had not met Fred Walbach before, and he tended to dislike the 'bulldozing' characteristics of many of the Americans he had met. He decided that he would stand his ground, however hard Walbach came on to him. His English wasn't bad but he needed time to think into English – or American? – phrases and behaviour patterns. But when all was said and done, he was the purchaser and should be in the stronger position.

Fred Walbach, Sales Director of Undersea Inc., was on the plane from

*Structure and Strategy*

San Francisco to Osaka – and had pulled out his lap-top to look at the notes he had made back at the Oakland office when he went to gen up on the technical discussions his colleagues had had with the men from KOK about the submersible. It seemed that KOK were happy with the technical details, and his notes looked clear.

## A. Data

- **Quoted price** $5.2 million (¥650 million) representing about a fifth of UI's turnover *(Note: We need this order!)*. A discount of 7½% could be given – reluctantly.
- **Delivery required** – 12 months *(Note: if agreed this would cut into our price: we'd prefer 14 months)*
- **Liquidated damages** *(How I hate liquidated damages, They're always charged to the Sales Division)* should be kept to 1% per week up to 5% max, against their demand for 2%.
- **Payment Terms**. We've quoted 30% with order and after 6 months, after a year, and 10% prior to delivery. *(Note: We need the money!)* They've muttered about total after delivery!
- **Guarantees**. We can only guarantee the sub for 12 months, and less where bought out parts carry less – then the cover is limited by the sub-contractor's contract.
- **Spares**. Separate quotation for $500k (¥60 million) for spares- agreed by KOK to be essential (Use Spares discount as a concession, – if unused we get them back!)

## B. Our Strengths

- KOK have informed us ours is the best spec. UI have been in the business now for 50 years including designing submarines for the US Navy. We are probably at this moment better than our competitors – though they are catching up fast. At present the dollar is very favourable against the Yen – which means that competitors from Europe are a very small threat.

## C. Objectives

- Long term. To try to build up a relationship which might bring more demands for submersibles in the future – means being pretty flexible on price.
- Short term. To get the contract signed on this visit – tempt Mr T to sign to-day!

## D. Strategy

- Try to discover early on his sticking points – are they price, delivery, payments or guarantees? – Is he a typical taciturn Japanese?

Mr Tamaka watched as Fred Walbach got out of the taxi and moved quickly into the shelter of the Osaka Tower. It was raining hard, a sort of monsoon rain they often had in August – no wind, just torrential rain, hour after hour.

After a few minutes, Tamaka moved out of his office to the lift to meet Walbach. The lift doors opened and Tamaka held out his hand as the square-built American came out without hesitation.

'Welcome to KOK, Mr Walbach,' he said. His English was smooth – he had spent two years in England studying language and electronics.

'Call me Fred.' Walbach's voice was flat and harsh. 'Your English is very good.' he said with a smile.

Tamaka ushered him into a cool conference room, where a young woman was waiting with a tray of tea and coffee.

'Coffee, please,' said Walbach as he moved to the table and unpacked his laptop.

'We have sockets here,' said Tamaka pointing to the wall, and sat down where the light would fall across Walbach's face. Tamaka believed in trying to judge Americans by their facial and body language. He looked at the papers in front of him – the technical ones were in English, the commercial ones in Japanese.

'Have you been to Japan before?' he asked.

'Sure. Many times, but never to Osaka. I mostly spent my time in Tokyo and took a vacation in Kyoto,' Walbach replied. 'You've a fine view from here.' Walbach looked out of the window.

'Would you like to start talking about the contract?' Tamaka was polite.

## Structure and Strategy

He had decided to disarm the American by apparently being pliable and compliant. 'Perhaps you'd better "set out your stall" as you say,' he went on.

'Thanks,' said Walbach, 'I thought we ought to talk about the delivery and the payment terms. If we get those out the way, the rest should be plain sailing.'

'You know our anxiety to have the sub in 12 months – and your quoted delivery is not really acceptable, at 14 months. Perhaps if we accepted 14 months you could reduce the price. After all, it would mean losing two months of our maintenance schedule. How about a 10% reduction in the price?'

Walbach stared at Tamaka – he didn't seem to be expecting to discuss the price this early in the conversation, and hadn't anticipated setting price against delivery time.

'I don't think ... um ... we could probably bring it in in 13 months. Would that solve the problem d'you think?'

'If you guaranteed that,' replied Tamaka, 'Then you could accept 2% liquidated damages. You could put some pressure on your people, couldn't you? – after five weeks you would be up to 10% anyway.'

Walbach is floundering now. He had hoped to take the whole negotiation at a gentle pace and would have liked to set the agenda. He gazes at the screen of his laptop without seeing it and realises he has been backed into a corner, and will have to lose 10% on the price whatever he does.

'Now, hang on, just a little minute, Mr Tamaka. I think you've got it all wrong. Can we take things gently? Perhaps we could agree an agenda – or a list of subjects we could then discuss. I, for my part, am most anxious that you should be comfortable with the contract I hope to sign with you.' He paused, 'What d'you say?'

Tamaka suddenly realised he was not dealing with a Driver – from his current stance he seemed to be more like an Amiable. So he looked back at his little booklet in his desk and saw that with an Amiable ... 'coffee, no rush, chit-chat, communicate patiently.'

'I'm so sorry,' he said. 'let's start again. I'm afraid I misjudged you – er, Fred.'

What he had done was to assume that Fred Walbach represented a stereotypical American salesman. But UI had recognised that, in their business, having Drivers (Controllers) as salesmen tended to antagonise customers.

'OK,' said Walbach, 'Could we begin with agreement that the technical specification is acceptable and that we have quoted 14 months delivery time for the agreed design of the submersible?'

Walbach had also realised that Tamaka was probably more like what his training would call a Processor – who needed a systematic approach, lots of facts and figures, and could not be rushed into a decision.

'Thank you,' said Tamaka, 'and I should, perhaps, stress that our priority is to obtain the sub in 12 months, as I said. If you can do that, I think we might be well on the way to looking at four more submersibles over the next five years.'

Fred Walbach swallowed hard and grinned.

'That's very interesting. Naturally we would be very anxious to quote for those. My problem with a twelve-month delivery is that it could be possible, but I can't shave a nickel off the price at all, much as I would like to. Can we perhaps agree on a twelve-month delivery at the quoted price of ¥650 million?'

'We, of course,' said Tamaka, 'have had very competitive quotations from competitors. Can you guarantee a 12-month delivery if we pay the full price?'

'Sure can,' said Fred.

'In that case, can we agree on the liquidated damages clause in the contract of 2% per week with a maximum of 10%?' Tamaka was relaxed.

'You drive a hard bargain, Mr Tamaka,' said Walbach, 'I shall have the greatest difficulty to sell not only a 12-month guaranteed delivery but heavy liquidated damages if we're late. I would be happy – well, not happy – but content, if we could come to some agreement about payment.'

'Can we leave the payment thing – just until we've ironed out a couple of other points, please?' said Tamaka gently.

'What would they be?' Walbach is now suspicious – he is afraid he may lose out, because the behaviour, the body language of Tamaka seems to him to demonstrate that he thinks he's winning.

'Just the guarantee on the submersible, could it be two years?'

'And what was the second thing?' Walbach queries. He's read the Italacom Case and noted the 'nibbling' strategy of Mr H in it. He is unwilling to be caught agreeing to one clause of the contract without getting something in return.

'The spares ...' Tamaka said. There was a period of silence. No one moved.

'So are you saying that a two-year guarantee and the spares are tied together?' Walbach has to be sure what Tamaka is attempting. 'Because,' he went on,' our problem is that we would like to give you a complete 2-year guarantee. Trouble is, we can't get even a 12-month guarantee from some of our sub-contractors. What I suggest is that we give you a 12-month guarantee to everything except for two or three items where the sub-contractor will only give a 4-month cover. How about that?' Walbach relaxed back into his chair and looked at his laptop. He had pushed the problem back to Tamaka who said nothing.

'If,' he said eventually, 'you can only guarantee the sub for 12 months we may have a greater need for spares. Would you consider charging for spares only after the end of the guarantee period – so that during that period you would provide them free, and after that we would pay for the spares at the price quoted?'

Walbach calculated that the cost to UI of a second year's guarantee would be more than the profit on the spares – and that there would be very little call for spares during the first year anyway. So he said, 'Can I give you my answer after we've discussed the payment terms?'

'Perhaps we should first write down what we've agreed so far,' said Tamaka, 'then we can haggle about payment terms.'

So they did. The balance of the payment terms came out acceptably fair to each party. And they agreed to review the terms if during the period the dollar and the yen changed their relationship more than 1% up or down.

They shook hands on the contract.

Tamaka took Walbach to lunch at a 'teppenyaki' restaurant where your food is chopped up and cooked in front of you on stainless steel hot plates. Walbach was very happy.

Should he have been?

*(Take a look at the case to see at what point Walbach 'assessed advantage' – and what did he do?)*

## The impasse

Perhaps we are stuck. Perhaps we are trying to negotiate with someone who just will not budge (Some Scandinavians tend to take that approach – what might be termed the 'Lutheran stance' – 'Here I stand! I can do no other!').

At this point, if you propose to continue, there are four possible courses of action.

- Make a new offer – once again, and naturally, defensible.
- Ask TOP for a new offer.
- Change the whole shape of the negotiation (see Walbach's approach above).
- Start 'give-and-take' bargaining (perhaps 'haggling' is nearer the mark).

It was the latter course that the sales people of Italacom took when faced with each of Mr H's demands. This resulted in, yes, a reduction in the severity of the demand, but this was all that Italacom got out of it on each occasion. Mr H made a demand for, say, 50. After haggling with Italacom he achieved, say, 25. Who is to say that this was not his original aim? And the same thing happened time and time again.

So the recommended course must be to rejig the offer, or like Walbach, change the whole direction of the offer. But then, as you will realise, Walbach was an Amiable and Tamaka an Analytical. As soon as each realised this, the whole atmosphere of the negotiation changed and the course of the negotiation was re-set. And the important phase of 'give-and-take' bargaining began.

We have now reached the point when the **list of concessions** created at the preparation stage comes into its own. But swapping concessions needs to have a few caveats attached.

- Concessions should be matched. *(In 'If I agree to this, will you agree to that'- 'this' and 'that', must have roughly equal value.)*
- The pace must be equal – do not shovel out a number of

## Structure and Strategy

concessions all at once – dribble them out as if from an eyedropper.

- Try to find a concession which is of low value to you to swap with one that is of high value to them. *('We can guarantee delivery provided you pay the full quoted price' – guaranteeing delivery cost you very little – getting full price is very valuable.)*

- Concessions should appear to be significant *('We will need to work very hard with our people to guarantee ...')* whereas concessions offered by TOP are 'mere icing on the cake'.

As part of the strategy, we need to be aware of the possibility of an impasse or a deadlock – and include in our planning some measures to escape from such an outcome. The first could be to bring in as many **variables** as possible. In the Italacom case, Mr H brought up the question of the accuracy of the metering of the flow of the raw material. The effect was further to delay the signing of the new contract.

Another possibility is to prepare an **escape route**.

The salesmen for a company selling double-glazing had a strategy for dealing with the problem of the cost of installation. They assumed that everyone wanted double-glazed windows and that the main obstacle would therefore be the cost. So they offered to arrange a relatively cheap loan to cover the cost – but then discussed the problem of repayment, not in terms of the total, but the possibility of monthly payments – *'how much can you afford, £120, £110 or just £100?'* – in effect challenging potential purchasers to demonstrate that they were better off than you might think. The block of the total price was thus carefully side-stepped – in fact, never mentioned. The whole 'sale' was about the monthly amount the customer could afford to pay.

A third measure to enable you to avoid the trap is to use **time breaks**, for tea, coffee or a drink, or start to talk about holidays, families, journeys or whatever. And, failing all else, try to change the whole mood of the meeting – move into what the Americans would call the 'golf club area' – *'Why don't we meet again for lunch and then* *go for a short trip on the river,'* or some such.

A final possibility – which, in industrial relations negotiations may well be a very early remedy – is to bring in a **third party**, an arbitrator, such as ACAS (the Advisory, Conciliation and Arbitration Service) which was set up to provide solutions to difficult industrial relations problems, in particular, to assist when deadlock is threatened.

The final section of the Structure has to do with **finalising agreement** (in the KOK Submersible Case, Tamaka says, *'Let's write down what we've agreed so far.'*)

As in a conventional selling situation, both parties should seek 'Final Agreement' as soon as possible. 'Buying Signals' (discussed in Chapter 5) should be watched for, such as: summarising, writing notes, closing books or laptops. What has been agreed must thus be clear to both parties; and neither should leave the negotiating area, conference room, office or whatever, without an agreement of some kind – if only on the date, time and place of the next meeting.

## Checklist for Chapter 4

- [ ] Is the lesson on structure from Italacom that one side was disciplined and followed a programme?

- [ ] Should a structure always be followed rigidly – or should the structure depend on events?

- [ ] Does the Submersible Case show that successful strategies depend on personality assessment?

- [ ] Was Fred Walbach happy because he had a satisfactory result – or just because he had a result?

- [ ] Do political negotiations such as Israel/Palestine have useful lessons for commercial negotiations – or is it the other way round?

- [ ] Who do you think would have won if Mr H from Polvercol had met Mr Tamaka from KOK – and why?

- [ ] List the strategies you have used or would find most usable.

# Listening questionnaire

**How good a listener are you?**

**Select with a tick one answer to each of the questions below and then add the score from the chart that follows.**

SCORE

1. Do you give the other party a chance to talk?
    a) Always  b) Sometimes  c) Rarely ☐

2. Do you interrupt while someone is making a point?
    a) Occasionally  b) Often  c) Never ☐

3. Do you look at the speaker when he/she is speaking?
    a) Most of the time  b) Sometimes
    c) Only when he/she is attractive ☐

4. Do you imply that your time is being wasted?
    a) Sometimes  b) Rarely  c) Very often ☐

5. Do you fidget with pencil or paper?
    a) Sometimes  b) Never ☐

6. Do you smile at the person talking to you?
    a) Only when a funny remark is made
    b) Most of the time  c) When I remember ☐

7. Do you try to get the speaker off track, or off the subject?
    a) Occasionally  b) Very often ☐

8. Are you open to new suggestions or do you react against them?
    a) Open  b) React against  c) Occasionally accept ☐

9. Do you jump ahead of the other person, anticipating his/her next point?
    a) Very often  b) Rarely
    c) Only when the other person is slow ☐

## Structure and Strategy

10. Do you try to put the other person on the defensive when you are asked a question?
    a) Rarely  b) Always  c) Never ☐

11. Do you ask questions which show you have not been listening?
    a) Regularly  b) Occasionally  c) Never ☐

12. Do you try to outstare the speaker?
    a) Yes  b) No ☐

13. Do you overdo your show of attention by nodding too much or saying 'yes' to everything?
    a) Sometimes  b) Only with people I like
    c) In difficult situations ☐

14. Do you insert humorous remarks when the other person is being serious?
    a) Never  b) Just to get him or her off balance
    c) Sometimes ☐

15. Do you sneak looks at your watch or the clock while listening?
    a) Only if the speaker is boring  b) Very rarely  c) Often ☐

    Total score ☐

## Listening score sheet

1. a) 5 b) 3 c) 1
2. a) 3 b) 1 c) 5
3. a) 5 b) 3 c) 1
4. a) 3 b) 5 c) 1
5. a) 1 b) 5

6. a) 3 b) 4 c) 1
7. a) 3 b) 1
8. a) 5 b) 1 c) 3
9. a) 2 b) 3 c) 5
10. a) 3 b) 1 c) 5

11. a) 1 b) 3 c) 5
12. a) 5 b) 1
13. a) 5 b) 1 c) 3
14. a) 5 b) 1 c) 3
15. a) 3 b) 5 c) 1

## Assessment of scores

| | |
|---|---|
| 65 – 72 | Good Listener |
| 42 – 65 | Not bad – but should make more effort |
| 20 – 42 | Must really try harder! |
| Below 20 | Deaf? |

# 5

# The Influence of Behaviour

'Shaking hands gives clues about the opposition' is perhaps a suitable starting point for a discussion of behaviour in the context of negotiation. For what we do influences the other party as much as what we say – and the way we say it often has more influence and effect than what we say.

In this chapter, the first part is therefore about non-verbal behaviour and interactive body language. The second part has to do with how emotion, humour and silence, among other actions, may be used to influence favourably the outcome of a negotiation, along with the recognition of buying signals and the use of behaviour to help your cause. *(At the beginning or the Hutton Enquiry in 2003, Lord Hutton forbade the presence of cameras and recording devices, because, he said, every hesitation, every apparent nervousness, every body movement by witnesses seen by cameras could be interpreted – or misinterpreted – by the TV viewer; and the very presence of cameras could inhibit some witnesses and distort their contribution.)*

To illustrate how non-verbal behaviour can influence negotiation, it is said that in the market places of the Middle East and the souks of Morocco, Algeria and Tunisia there comes a point in the 'haggling' when the potential 'buyer' starts to walk away, to signal there is to be no deal. This action in itself does not impress the seller. But tradition holds that when a customer has walked 30 paces, he or she will not return. So if the merchant is willing to offer a better price or deal he waits until the customer had gone 28 paces or so and then he runs after him or her. Nothing needs to be said. There is no shouting of such phrases as 'Come back!' or 'You'll not know what you're missing!' – simply a receding back.

Another illustration of the use of body language only is of the lecturer I knew who was never troubled by questions at the end of his lecture. When asked how he managed it he said: *'I always finish my talk about two minutes before the hour is up, and then ask whether there are any questions. At that point I always look away from the audience and start to collect up my papers and visual aids. Strangely enough I am very rarely troubled with questions!'*

A very large amount of research has been done into Body Language – not least by Desmond Morris, recorded in 'Man Watching'. There has even been a study of human behaviour in conflict (battle) which has shown that the prime movers of the individual soldier are 'personal survival' and the fear of 'the group's contempt for failure or apparently cowardly action.' An indication of what might happen when even in straightforward negotiation one of the parties fears he has his back to the wall.

## Eye contact

One of the most important of what might be called non-verbal indicators is eye contact. Eye contact, it is said, has a pattern which is intuitively recognised as necessary and desirable in a relationship. Try this small experiment – look hard at someone as you ask them a question and continue to look at them as they answer, then try the same question on another person, but this time don't look at that person as they answer. What variations are there in either their speed of response or enthusiasm? When you looked at them, they would probably respond quickly and thoughtfully. When you did not look at them while they answered, their response was probably casual and uninterested. Notice, if you attend a talk, a lecture or a sermon, that if the speaker looks at you from time to time, you will pay more attention than if he or she either reads the talk or gazes at the ceiling or looks into the middle distance.

Where memory is concerned, it is said that if you are trying to remember something visual, subconsciously your eyes will look *up to the left*; when you are trying to remember words or sounds, your eyes look directly to the left; and when you are trying to remember something conceptual your eyes tend to look *downward to the left*. Similarly when trying to create an image, you will look *up to the right*, when trying to imagine words or sounds, *directly right*, and when trying to imagine feelings, *down to the right*.

This is best explained by a simple illustration.

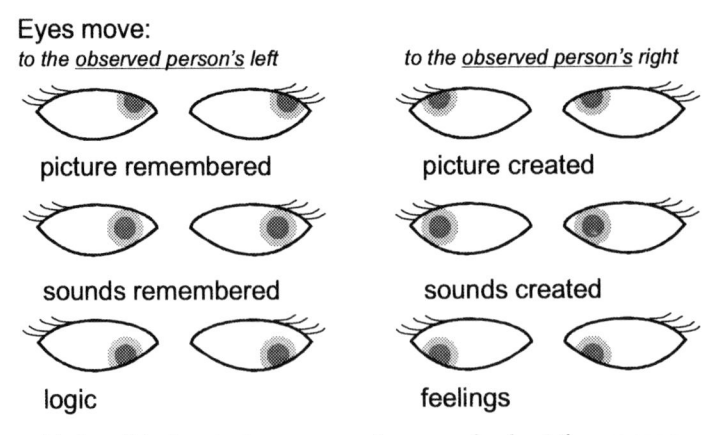

**Eyes move:**

| to the <u>observed person's</u> left | to the <u>observed person's</u> right |
|---|---|
| picture remembered | picture created |
| sounds remembered | sounds created |
| logic | feelings |

**Note** - this is what you see when you look at the person

This is generally true for right-handed people, the opposite is usually found with left-handed people. Remember though that this is quite a broad generalisation, but it can be helpful in assessing the thinking processes of the person you are talking to.

Eye contact between two people, however, needs careful management. In a general conversation between two people who are acquainted, research has shown that there may be a norm of about 6 to 8 eyeball-to-eyeball contacts of some 3/4 of a second each, per minute. Of course this amount of eye contact varies with the nature of the two negotiators. Ideally, when you are making a comment or asking a question, you need to look at the other party every so often to see how he or she is taking what you have to say – whether TOP is bored, surprised, outraged, sneering, thinking hard or just waiting for you to finish. One can usually tell whether he or she is listening from his or her eyes. *(I have a friend who always takes off her spectacles to demonstrate that she is listening to you and is not otherwise distracted.)* So, when the other party is talking, you need to give him or her your full and undivided attention – and can demonstrate this by looking directly at the eyes. Negotiators are often advised to keep free of the distraction of detailed papers – to use cards with headings as memory joggers – so that eyes can be used to observe the other party's eyes and other body language.

## Body language or kinesics*
(*The study of non-verbal communication using the methods and concepts of American descriptive linguistics of the late 1940s.)

Body language can be divided (for analytical purposes), into two sections – the body language which you can consciously use – your posture, your stance and your gestures – and the body language which is an unconscious indicator of a state of mind. The latter is far more difficult to interpret, and has become a hunting ground for anthropologists.

The first could be termed part of interactive body language, because you are consciously trying to have an effect by something you do: a good starting point might be posture. 'An alert posture influences the other party; a slouching position gives a different impression' – a sentence found among the tips for a negotiator. Unexceptional, but what does it mean for the ordinary person?

Perhaps if we 'stand up straight and don't lounge about' we will give an impression of inflexibility – do we want to do that? Do we want to go into a play-acting mode, 'so as to deceive our opponent'? There was a time, many years ago, when biscuit salesmen of Huntley and Palmer had to wear dark suits, white shirts and bowler hats – and a job applicant who turned up smartly dressed in tweeds and a pork pie hat was rejected. (It must have been a long time ago – to-day's readers may never have seen a bowler or a pork pie hat except in old black and white films!)

The question therefore arises, in relation to posture – how should we present ourselves? – as honest and straightforward? – that is assuming we *are* straightforward and honest. The difficulty which arises is that however we disguise our appearance (our posture for example), if we are going to be negotiating over any period of time – from half-an-hour upwards – such masks as we may have donned will inevitably have slipped – and our true selves will have been revealed.

Taking the 'Submersible Case' as an example, Mr Tamaka, an Analytical, was clearly chosen for his job for his qualities as a Procurement Manager. You would not expect him to become a 'hail-fellow-well-met' suddenly. Nor, therefore, could Fred Walbach suddenly turn into a Driver. So the body language of each will probably quite early indicate their basic behaviour patterns. The Analytical will probably be precise in his movements, posture and dress. Fred Walbach, the Amiable, will be more relaxed both in his body movement and in his dress; the description 'smart casual' might well have been devised for people like Fred.

Nevertheless, it is important to realise that posture is an important indicator – a non-verbal indicator – of the sort of person we are – or the kind of impression we wish to make. *(Many years ago, I told my secretary that I admired how she stood and moved. 'My father sent me to deportment classes,' she said, 'they would help me to get a better job, he said.' Her posture certainly made one give her a second glance!)*

Gestures seem to span the gap between conscious non-verbal language and unconscious body language. Having for a number of years taught the skills of presentation to those who believed they needed it for their job and to those who thought they knew all about 'presentation', I have long recognised that one of the major problems people have is the use of gesture. The book of 'tips' says simply that 'gestures can reinforce messages'. Yes, certainly they can if used consciously, but they can also distract. *(A famous example of the latter was Alastair Campbell when he went into Channel 4 Studios to protest. He became very angry about something and his gesture consisted, not, conventionally, of a fist banging the table, but of holding a pencil upright, and banging the table with the side of his* hand. *The camera was focused on the gesture – and kept returning to it, making it a sort of distraction from what Campbell was saying, and diminishing the importance of his protest.)*

The first thing the negotiator needs to do is to discover, from a friend, which gestures he or she unconsciously makes.*(One of the TV 'weather girls' has a gesture of opening both her hands at the end of each sentence – tempting watchers to count how many times she does it – about five times in three minutes – and to miss the important weather forecast.)* Secondly, the putative negotiator should try to work out what conscious gestures come easily – and what remarks they reinforce. Here is a list of remarks and suitable gestures to go with them.

| Remark | Gesture |
| --- | --- |
| 'I'm afraid that's the best I can do.' | Both hands palm up |
| 'Is that all you can offer?' | Lift right eyebrow (or left if easier) |
| 'What you're asking is impossible.' | Right fist gently on the table |
| 'I'm sorry, but I just said ...' | Fist twice on the table |
| 'This is the complete solution to the ...' | Both hands wide |
| 'I think you know more than that'. | Head on one side |
| 'What about improving your offer ...' | Right hand open |
| 'Come on: you've said that already.' | Hands behind head |
| 'Yeah, yeah, yeah, I would agree' | Nod vigorously |
| 'I simply cannot see a way round that ...' | Shaking head, pursed lips |
| 'Now you're talking ...' | Big, wide, toothy smile |
| 'This has gone on too long already.' | Rest cheek on hand |
| 'You really expect me to believe that?' | Eyes up to heaven |
| 'I'll have to think about it.' | Smoothes hair (or bald scalp!) |
| 'Great! I agree!' | Both hands open, in front of face |
| 'I'll have to think about that ...' | Pursed lips, frown |
| 'I really don't understand you.' | Slow head-shake |
| 'There's really nothing more to be said!' | Stare, pursed lips, unmoving. |

I do not suggest taking this list with you on a card into the negotiation, but try them out in front of a mirror or with a friend.

It is more difficult trying to relate some aspects of body-language to their meaning, since certain unconscious body movements may be peculiar to the person with whom you are negotiating. Nevertheless, for the sake of completeness it maybe useful to list the accepted view of a number of fairly obvious non-verbal indications. To quote Tim Hindle in *'Negotiating Skills', 'learning to read body language among the opposition team will help you to compile a true picture of their case – their signals may reinforce or contradict what they are saying.'*

With that warning in mind, here are some of the possible indications body language may give.

| Indicator | Sign |
| --- | --- |
| Finger tapping | Irritation, impatience at delay or hesitation by TOP |
| Blink rate increase | Apprehension of disaster or unacceptable suggestion |
| Crossing legs (male) | Defensive reaction to attack |
| Crossing legs (female) | Possibly suggestive or giving in |
| Slumping in seat | Recognition that the 'battle' is lost |
| Looking away | Same as above or confusion as to what's happening |
| Visible bodily relaxation | We are winning |
| Sitting on the edge of one's seat (lumbar tension) | We are on the winning straight |

Once again, the trainee negotiator should do some research among kinsfolk and acquaintance to check this list's applicability.

## The voice

From *The Times* leader about the life of Sir Edward Pickering, a famous newspaper editor, *'a quizzical look or a deceptively mild aside sufficed to prompt a colleague to question the wisdom of a news judgement or the solidity of a story'*. Note a 'deceptively mild aside' because where the voice is concerned it is not only what we say but the way we say it. So I examine the use of the voice under a number of headings, the first being **emphasis**. Try saying, 'How are you to-day?' several times, emphasising a different word each time.

- 'How are <u>you</u> to-day?' You are the most important person to the speaker at that moment; which is quite different from ...
- 'How are you <u>to-day</u>?' – as against yesterday or some days ago.
- 'How <u>are</u> you to-day?' when a few days ago you seemed to be quite ill.
- '<u>How</u> are you to-day?' – means how do you feel in yourself.

If there are such subtleties in a four word sentence, how many more are there likely to be when what we are saying can vary with how we say it. So the first point about the voice is that we can give emphasis to words and phrases which is not possible in written communication except with the rather clumsy use of underlining, italics or exclamation marks. (The current use of text messages on mobile/cell phones must restrict the possibility of using emphasis in any subtle way.)

    The second category of the use of the voice has to do with the **pace of delivery**. I had a Dutch friend whose English was perfect – so perfect in fact that I advised him to make himself a notice for his lectern which read 'SLOWLY AND CLEARLY'. Very often it takes some time for strangers to get used to your accent and pronunciation (think about Mr Tamaka and Fred Walbach). There are some whose words pour out at such a rate even their friends may not take in every word. Mind you, taking it too slowly can also be considered by your audience – the other party – to be insulting. Along with 'pace' we may also weigh up the **use of words**. It is always easier to use short words whose meaning is not in doubt rather than polysyllabic monsters which can easily confuse your opponent. (Try using 'gubernatorial election' as a description of the contest for governor in an American state, as heard recently in a BBC account – perfectly correct but overly pedantic.) The strategy as described in Chapter 4 must be 'to speak to be understood' – and I might add 'not to demonstrate your own cleverness'.

A third variable with the voice has to do with **pitch** or level and power or **volume**. A certain amount of initial nervousness will cause a rise in the pitch of the voice (from bass to tenor, let us say, to use a musical analogy). After the first few minutes, your natural conversational pitch should take over. Changes in power or volume should remain under your control and can be used to create some effect: if you wish strongly to emphasise a point.

'I think it is very important that you should be clear about our policy on this subject,' said quietly would not make the impact that it would if you put it in vocal capital letters. 'I THINK THAT YOU SHOULD BE CLEAR ABOUT OUR POLICY ON THIS SUBJECT' *(Do not, however, be fazed by the automatic response from Call Centre employees if you raise your voice above a whisper in order to reiterate a point which the respondent has consistently not understood – 'Please don't be rude!' or 'I don't answer people who are rude!' – making the assumption that emphasis is of itself 'rude', or it may be that they have been trained that if you call a person 'rude' it will put that person at a disadvantage. You should continue to negotiate.)* Emphasis can also be demonstrated by talking more slowly; care must be taken to avoid the accusation of being insulting.

Finally, by tactical use of **pauses**, one can often gain or regain the initiative: 'D'you think it would be at all possible to ... well ... perhaps ... um ... improve your initial ... um ... offer by ... about, say, for the sake of argument ... um ... ten percent or ... ?' By the time you've finished asking the question, TOP is slightly confused as to whether you are asking for too much or making a tentative attempt to achieve agreement. Thus the pause can cause TOP either to rush ahead to his or her answer or to give a response unconnected with the question.

*(I had a boss once whose view it was that nobody answered the question they were asked. When I disagreed, he suggested we take a bet on it, to which I agreed. He called in his secretary and said to her, 'How much did you pay for that frock?' She answered, 'I bought it in Lewis's'. I paid up.)*

Perhaps a total **silence** may well prove advantageous. Here is an illustration from possible dialogue in the Submersible Case.

1. Tamaka   'Surely you can improve your delivery from 14 months to 12 months'

    Walbach   'Well, we really cannot do that, because we are having great difficulty in meeting the deliveries that we've already promised, and the costs of doing this would be pushed up by overtime we would have to work, and there are problems of inflation anyway which cause us to be in great difficulty cost-wise, and we know from previous experience what will happen if we ...'

2. Tamaka   'Surely you can improve your delivery from 14 months to 12 months'

    Walbach   'No ......!'

Silence here has the advantage that it pushes the whole argument back to Tamaka – whereas if Walbach tries to justify his stance, he just stumbles around and loses the initiative.

## Humour and emotion

Coleridge wrote, *'No mind is thoroughly well organised that is deficient in a sense of humour.'* Colette remarked, *'Total absence of humour renders life impossible'*. Wittgenstein claimed that his ambition to write a philosophical work constructed entirely of jokes was frustrated when he realised he had no sense of humour, (Introduction to the *Oxford Dictionary of Humorous Quotations* by Ned Sherrin). Finally, to quote EV Lucas, *'In England, it is very dangerous to have a sense of humour.'*

However, most 'Lonely Hearts' ads contain the abbreviation GSOH (good sense of humour) either being sought or being offered, which would often seem to be a rather more important feature than looks or wealth. In negotiation, it is more valuable as a useful distracting tool – not that you should feel it important to drop in a couple of jokes. However funny they may be, they should be kept for the pub or the lunch table. Humour can bring a change of pace, a relaxation of tension or a fresh perspective on a problem. It could be a witty comment arising from the discussion or a view of the absurdity of a situation.

One of the main findings of researchers working on the way groups coped with problems is the way in which the tension generated by the group is released – most often by laughter, following a humorous comment made by a member of the group. In negotiation, humour can best be used in two ways – as a genuine release of tension, when it is felt by both parties that it is time for a break, or as a stalking horse under the guise of which one party is trying to get the other to lower his or her guard. *(Come to think of it, this last is probably one of the tricks used by the aforementioned 'Lonely Heart' to get his or her wicked will!)*

Humour can also be used to diffuse or disarm emotion. The union leader who remarked angrily that an offer from an employer 'had more strings than the Royal Philharmonic' was using humour and emotion together to make a powerful point. Emotion is often demonstrated by greater articulation, the use of vigorous expressions including swearing – and perhaps appealing to finer or deeper feelings. As mentioned earlier, in Britain we tend to be less open with our personal feelings, the demonstration of which is not 'what a real man should do' – a 'real man' bottles up his feelings, and presents a 'stiff upper lip'. *(Though as someone said, a 'stiff upper lip' may be accompanied by a 'slack lower jaw!')*

Strong emotion often demonstrates that the other party has a personal stake in a certain aspect of the negotiation – perhaps something is the negotiator's 'baby', and he or she feels very strongly about a particular line of action, or will defend to the last his or her right to do, to have, to keep something. And it is very difficult to find a realistic, or down-to-earth, way round an emotional obstacle of this strength. One of the useful tactics of a negotiator is to try to expose a sore or emotional part of the subject as early as possible, so as to defuse it or negotiate it away early on. 'I'm sorry I didn't realise you were so stuck on ...' is often too late a comment to have any effect. It is also true to say that a break may help emotions to cool so as to continue negotiations later in a less emotionally charged atmosphere.

## Buying signals

One of the major parts of conventional sales training is the recognition of 'buying signals' – trying to assess whether the potential customer has made a buying decision by recognising certain signals both in speech and body language. Similar signals occur during negotiations and can demonstrate that TOP may have agreed to a certain course of action – possibly before it is clear to TOP-self. For example, he or she smiles or even looks out of the window – the kind of satisfied gesture which tells you (as a salesperson) that TOP has decided to go along with your offer. (Beware of the old trap: the offerer suggests, say, that he will lower the price to £5,000. You are delighted and accept the offer – but you then suddenly realise from the look on his face that he would have been prepared to go down to £4,000!)

Mr Tamaka (of KOK) might start to talk about future co-operation. *'When we have tested the 'sub' in the sea out there, perhaps we should talk about the future. Will you be coming to Japan regularly, d'you think?'* – a clear buying signal for the current contract, even though there may be a few things to be ironed out. It would though be a great mistake for Fred Walbach to think that this is a discussion of future business – it refers only to Tamaka giving a buying signal about the sale of the first submersible.

There are also a couple of physical buying signals you should look out for. The putative purchaser of some physical product may pick up the 'sample' – showing that he or she now feels a degree of ownership and will most likely buy it. *(Sales people with samples have usually been trained to have at least two identical ones. If the sales person puts down one as a demonstrator, the buyer will not pick it up, as the 'owner' is still the sales person – if, however, there are two identical ones, the buyer is prepared to feel what it would be like to own the product. No car salesman would ever offer to drive a buyer or even sit anywhere but in the passenger seat – or even the back seat – in the car he is trying to sell.)* In a negotiation, 'ownership' can be indicated by the closing of a notebook, shutting the laptop – moving to a different area of conversation. You need to watch and listen carefully to pick up signs. (Check 'How Good a Listener are You?' quiz in Chapter 4)

*(Experience in a number of training courses where video role playing had been used shows that many of those whose opponents had 'given in' continued to press when they had already won as much as possible.)*

There are several further 'buying signals'.

- First, the beginning of discussion about credit terms (see Double Glazing salesmen above!).

- Second, TOP starts to talk about the need for guarantees (look back to the Submersible Case). If your product is made to the highest standards, than giving a guarantee is one of the cheapest concessions which can be offered.

- Third, TOP begins to worry about levels of service – 'do you provide preventive maintenance or breakdown service' is a question which might be posed to the provider of Health Insurance for the staff and gives a clear signal that the Human Resources manager has taken ownership of the service offered.

- And last but not least, asking for a price reduction or increased discount for cash, say, is often a clear indication that the buyer has decided on the purchase.

## Active interaction

In the Video Arts film *'Negotiating Profitable Sales'*, one of the trainers remarks, 'Never give a concession. Trade it reluctantly.' This principle can be translated into body language in two ways – over-valuing concessions given, and under-valuing concessions offered by the other party. Of course you will have decided what to say about the concession you are offering – *'I can only even offer this after a great deal of argument and discussion with my people ...'* or when TOP offers one – *'Is that the best you can do ...?'*

But you can reinforce or over-value your concession by putting some more excitement into your voice; and undervaluing his or her concession by looking straight at TOP, or by an exaggerating gesture (see earlier tables), such as a worried frown of a swift intake of breath. *(Listen sometime to the second-hand car salesman when you suggest to him the price you hope to get for your car. He is the master of undervaluing your idea. He walks away, kicks the tyres, sucks his teeth and sighs. By the end of his performance you wonder whether your car is worth anything at all, and would be glad to accept anything.)*

In the more sophisticated surroundings of a negotiation, you can also undervalue any concession offered by the other party either by reinforcing a remark such as *'That's not very important.'* with a superior smile, or, having listened carefully to TOP's description of the concession, you say nothing but simply turn away, or give a dismissive hand gesture, as if, perhaps you are waving away a fly. Or, even more dismissively, simply ignore what TOP has said and change the subject, and talk about something else. *(A friend of mine found this technique very useful when dealing with kitchen and bathroom salespeople. About half-way through a presentation, he would ask 'How old are you?' Such an sudden change of subject had a tendency to disorient the sales presenter. My friend recommended changing the subject in this way as a very useful technique for avoiding making unkind or rude comments on the concession offered.)*

Development of an undervaluing technique should also involve practising the 'superior smile' meaning, to quote Shakespeare, *'I could an if I would'*, meaning 'You don't know what I could do if I put my mind to it.'

Equally important in training to be a successful negotiator are some suggestions of ways of bringing pressure to bear on the other party and how to upset TOP – if that's what you want to do. Such behaviour would be needed when you find yourself 'losing the battle', and may, as a last resort, prevent the whole negotiation turning into a rout. But they can also be used when it appears from TOP's body language that he or she is aware that you are winning, but needs to be pushed harder to acknowledge this. (I recommend initial practice on friends or colleagues!)

To bring pressure to bear, you can try 'staring' or 'stillness' – the former may well produce to-day's fashionable demand, the accented 'Wha--at?' Stillness can very often tempt TOP to make anew offer. You can also try 'leaning forward' (now known in some quarters as the 'Alastair-Campbell-position') to make your point more emphatically, or give vocal support by repeating the sentence more slowly or more loudly or both. Sometimes the use of a 'poker face' – the 'neither confirm or deny' approach, may well come across to TOP as 'forcing' (If you play Bridge, you can practise non-verbal actions on your partner. It might help!)

Finally, if you really are determined to upset your opponent, you can try the second-hand car salesman's 'swift intake of breath', followed by, *'You thought how much?'* Incredulity is often a cause of upset. *'I just can't believe you are asking me/us to accept this level of cost when you ...'* Indeed you can stretch this idea to: *'Perhaps you should check your calculations; I reckon that you can still knock a further 5% off the price ...'* and to round off, back to the smiling superiority, *'Yes, we all know where you're coming from; we've all been there – and we know ...'*

The title of a book by Julius Fast called *'Body Language'* has a strap line, 'Your body doesn't know how to lie'. This chapter has described some of the underlying processes by which we can understand and perhaps counteract body language and interact with it.

## Checklist for Chapter 5

- [ ] Do we recognise the difference between conscious and unconscious body language?

- [ ] Have you checked whether your posture is indicative of your character? And are you happy with it?

- [ ] What kinds of gesture do you currently use? Have you practised gestures connecting to your speech?

- [ ] Are you aware of the indicators of unconscious body language?

- [ ] Are you happy to use techniques to bring pressure to bear on TOP?

# 6

# Team Negotiating

For large projects which may have a number of different sections, different technologies, or different time-scales, the negotiation needs to be carried out by a Team. The problems of negotiating as a team with other teams or with individuals are different in many respects from the problems discussed earlier in the one-to-one negotiations. Perhaps the first and most difficult problem is to ensure that the team behaves as a team – thus like a choir rather than a group of soloists, or a football team rather than a group of brilliant individual players

## Team negotiating characteristics

The essential characteristics of team negotiation can include:

- the size of the group
- the control of the team
- team leadership
- strategic considerations.

In the first place, the need for a team rather than an individual most often arises from the fact that one person cannot contribute sufficient expertise or knowledge to the negotiation, or there is no one person who can accept responsibility for all the implications affecting the outcome. As will be evident from the Elto Case Study, the different specialities each required a team member, both on the side of the client, Elto, and on the part of the proposed contractor FABRIKO. (see page 115).

Accepted practice states that the absolute number susceptible to control and able to be of value in a negotiating situation is eight. Because of the need to control the team and not to overwhelm the other party with too many different views, experience shows that the best number is probably four. With this number, a compact group can be created which will not allow the other party to isolate one or other member of the team from the rest – and attempt to undermine him or her.

There may, however, still be circumstances where more specialist knowledge or information is needed; this can be acquired by agreeing a recess ('time out') or by changing the membership of the team (using football parlance – 'bringing on a substitute' – and since there are no referees or linesmen, no one will be able to check on the studs in his or her boots!).

Teams, and particularly ad hoc teams, can be very difficult to control. The difficulty usually arises from the team's composition rather than its numbers. If it is necessary to provide the team with both the appropriate specialist knowledge and level of responsibility, you may have to use someone who feels that he or she ought to have greater authority than can be allowed to a member of the team. This problem shows up in the ELTO case study where the factory manager who leads the Elto Team is lower in rank than the deputy financial director of the company; the latter is often tempted to overrule the former.

Successful team negotiating therefore requires at least some training in how to present information (the notorious *'Iraq Dossier'* of 2003 comes to mind!) so that your case is clear. Your team also needs to discuss and agree on negotiation strategies and tactics (as outlined in earlier Chapters) so that individuals understand the way in which the Team Leader is trying to steer the negotiation. And, of course, training in aspects of teamwork. Selection boards for the Civil Service, building on the experience of Army selection boards in

World War II, very often try to assess a candidate's ability and attitude towards working in a team by giving a group a task which can only be accomplished if the members co-operate as a team. Those candidates who are extremely competitive by nature are usually not good team players: such attitudes need to be recognised in the creation of a negotiating team.

## Leading – problems and strategies

There is no single style of leader to suit all circumstances (outstanding examples are war leaders and peace leaders – 'destroyers' and 'builders' perhaps?) The Team Leader must naturally command respect from the members of the team – probably should be of a similar level or standing as the Leader of the other party – and must be thoroughly au fait with negotiating tactics.

Qualities of 'leadership' have been, and still are, much discussed and debated. Good leadership often depends on the qualities and attributes of the 'followers'. It certainly depends on the willingness of the leader not only to delegate but to delegate the most appropriate aspects of leadership to one or other of the 'followers'. It has been argued that leaders are often either 'action' people or 'thinking and planning' people – and that they therefore need some complementary functionary. Action leaders usually need an 'éminence grise' to look after the 'planning and thinking' functions – and vice versa. (It is said that we are all partly one and partly the other – 80% action and 20% planning or 80% planning and 20% action)

The leader needs to understand, in all circumstances, the principles of the team members' specialisations. Moreover, the characteristics of team members may well affect the operation of the team – and the leader needs to be aware of them. (Extensive discussion of these matters is given earlier in Chapter 3.) Even more important, perhaps, is the fact that the leader needs to specify the tasks and role of each team member for the duration of the negotiation, recognising that these may differ from their daily role.

Even if the leader has prepared both him- or herself, there are a number of common problems which arise during a 'team negotiation'. Many of them are the result of sloppy preparation – but many also arise from lack of elementary discipline in the team.

- The former include a lack of team discussion of an agreed negotiating strategy – how are we going to tackle this problem, what are our objectives, what do we hope to achieve, how long do we expect the meeting to last, will it be worth while having a break for tea? These are the sort of questions which must be answered before the negotiation commences. Otherwise some bright spark may bring up one or other of the questions half-way through, whispering to the team leader. A problem can also arise because a specialist is not aware of the negotiation tactics and therefore may find some of them 'unethical'.

- In looking for weaknesses in their opponents, teams may pick on particular specialists and try to undermine them by, for example, casting doubt on their knowledge of the speciality represented, or disagreeing with an expert opinion, or suggesting that later research has shown the opposite to be the case! A counter to such tactics might well be part of the leader's preparation – such as an immediate subject change when such an attack seems to be developing.

- By contrast, team members may disagree among themselves as the negotiation proceeds. This can happen as a result of a team member's assessment of risk or likelihood differing from that of team colleagues. A specialist may disagree with another member of the team about a point outside his or her specialist knowledge. Once again the leader would need to take immediate action to restore the position, by insisting on his or her authority.

- Two further problems can arise. One is that, even though team members do not verbally interrupt, they pass notes to the Team Leader, commenting either on points which should have been raised or rebutting the other party's arguments – both of which may distract the Leader from following the planned (and agreed) strategy line.

- Finally – and most upsetting – team members show that they are unaware of the stages of the negotiation (*'Yes! I agree, but we covered that point ten minutes ago!'*).

Most strategies and negotiating techniques have been covered in earlier chapters – and in team negotiating they will largely be the same. There are some others which are specific to team negotiations.

- The first of these is the tactic of concentrating on the weakest member of the other party's team, and trying to discommode him or her. This tactic often has the effect of destabilising the opposing team.

- A second method which tends to upset the other party's team is to direct the answer to a Team Leader's question at a specialist. *'What are your deadlines on this building?' 'That depends on the date you, Mr Architect, can provide us with detailed blueprints!'*

- A third tactic involves calling a 'recess' at a point where deadlock threatens or where difficult demands are made. Examples of this tactic are legion in political or industrial negotiations.

- A fourth point is the principle that the strongest member of the team, regardless of speciality, should deal with the most difficult situation.

To illustrate the kinds of situation which can arise, here is a case where there is a need for a team to negotiate on both sides.

## The Elto Case – team negotiating

The Elto Company, which currently manufactures Printed Circuit Boards in a factory of around 3,000 sq. metres (with technology of up to 24 layers down to 5 thou T&G) has decided to extend its factory by around 600 sq. meters to accommodate both chip placing machines and a new CAD/CAM centre for the design and production of electronic components.

In the new extension, the factory management together with the works council want to include alongside the factory a small warehouse with a loading bay, and a supervisory and design office block and changing rooms for the 45 staff who will be working in the new extension. (The factory area will need to have to have a 'pure environment').

Although the main contractor has been chosen (Fabriko Corp) largely because they have worked for Elto before, the final contract has not been signed and the meeting today is arranged between teams from Elto and Fabriko in order to iron out matters. Both sides want to agree in principle (initial the contract) so that the final details can be put in hand as soon as possible. The land purchase was already made at the time when the factory was first built – ten years ago

The Elto team comprises Arthur Smart, the Factory Manager, Clyde Winston, financial manager, Doreen Fitzgeorge, the Personnel Manager and John Warburton, a consultant whose background is as a quantity surveyor. The only one who has had experience of negotiating on Elto's behalf was Arthur Smart, so it was agreed that he was to be the Team Leader. They all knew the Team Brief (above) which had been drawn up by the Managing Director and Arthur Smart. Each member was then asked to draw up in writing a preparation document from the point-of-view of his or her own expertise.

Arthur Smart, as factory manager, has three or four objectives, some sticking points and some slight anxieties about certain aspects of Fabriko's approach and management of sub-contractors. Added to which, he suspects that the consultant, John Warburton ( whom Smart privately considers a 'clever clogs'), may well need some firm handling.

## Arthur's five objectives were as follows:

1) Production in the new extension must be up and running by the beginning of the next financial year. This would mean that, allowing for some slippage, the whole factory should be ready for production in nine months' time.

2) Machinery ordering had already been put in hand to be ready for installation in six months.

3) To keep Warburton from having detailed discussions about construction techniques which should be held after the contract is signed.

4) To ensure that Clyde Winston only shows price flexibility as a last resort and doesn't keep offering his opinions.

5) To establish regular joint monitoring of progress with Fabriko.

Clyde Winston, financial manager, who is also deputy to the Financial Director, had very clear ideas of how the negotiation should proceed. Elto had made provision for £640K for the main building (or 'shell and core') and £35K for internal fittings. He reckoned they could depreciate these amounts over the next 10-12 years and the profit from the new extension would cover the extra interest. He also felt that Fabriko's quotation for the building was too high – probably an opening bid. His view of the 'fitting out' quotation was that some of Fabriko's competitors could certainly do the job more cheaply, and that this should be used to force Fabriko to lower their price.

Doreen Fitzgeorge, the Personnel Manager, who is always likely to take the side of the work-force in any dispute, is anxious that the disruption of the existing factory does not cause upset among the staff. She would also insist that works' representatives are involved in the planning of the interior fittings. and she is concerned that the start of the new building (i.e. the greatest part of the disruption) be delayed until the beginning of the annual holiday and maintenance shut-down.

John Warburton, the consultant, who has been asked to advise on the detailed costing provided by Fabriko and the quality standards of the work, is also anxious to establish dates and times of inspection and agreement on the levels of quality acceptable in the 'pure environment'.

## Team Negotiating

Arthur Smart reckons his major team problems will arise from Doreen Fitzgeorge's interventions (what he calls her 'what about the workers?' bleats) and from the stubbornness of Clyde Winston on prices and costs. John Warburton always likes to be asked – Arthur reckons he can always create a diversion by asking for John's opinion. Otherwise, he believes he can reach his objectives.

The Fabriko team comprises a Project Manager (Harold Endicott) a Quantity Surveyor (Wilf Finch), the Commercial Manager (Andrew Surtees) and the 'fitting out' Manager (Deirdre Manton). The four know each other quite well, and have worked together on previous projects. According to Harold Endicott, this should give them an 'edge' against the Elto team, which, as he says, is just a 'scratch bunch'! Indeed Harold has no difficulty in running the Fabriko team, being dominant by nature.

His objectives are divided into five. He has discussed each with one of team members.

**Delivery:** to agree seven months for the basic building from an agreed starting date and a nine month completion – which would include Fabriko doing the 'fitting out' (Wilf Finch believes that if ELTO were to employ a separate company for the 'fitting out' the job would take longer even though it might be cheaper).

**Price:** Our opening bid will be £770K for the 'shell and core' plus £35K for the 'fitting out'. If the whole job were to be handled by us then we might be able to squeeze it down to £690K. There had been some argument with Deirdre about the price and the quality of 'fitting out'. She had pointed out that her sub-contractors were by a long way the best in the business – and had had quite a bit of experience in hi-tech factories. But Harold had convinced her that he would be able to negotiate an adequate profit for her.

**Access:** The objective was to start as soon as possible and to make the quoted price dependent on getting immediate access. The team reckoned that any disruption to the work in the factory would only become a nuisance in the third week, when the existing wall had to be breached to create connections.

**Disruption costs:** The Fabriko team realised that Elto would try to put them under pressure to complete construction and so on in the shortest possible time. Their 'bread and butter' was at stake. This would mean that Deirdre's people might have to work overtime. The team was firm that any overtime must be paid for by the client.

**Payment:** The team was experienced in trying to get clients to pay as early as possible – interest on borrowed money was a burden. Normal in the trade was monthly payment after the quantity surveyor had priced the work done. And if payment was then delayed, a standard penalty of 1% per month would be invoked. With 'fitting-out', Deirdre was firm, requiring 75% payment on completion, with 25 % a month later – because of having to pay sub-contractors' and suppliers' bills. This would carry a penalty of 1% per month for late payments.

Harold Endicott, after discussion with his Team, created a table showing what Fabriko expected from the two parties to the Negotiation.

## Negotiating Areas

| Areas | ELTO | FABRIKO |
|---|---|---|
| Delivery | 6 months machinery in 9 months completion | 7 months "shell and core" 9 months completion including "fitting out" |
| Price | £675K    £640K "s & c" £35K "fitting out" | Try for £770K "s & c" £35K "fitting out" £690K 'whole job' |
| Access | 2 weeks at the beginning | Immediate access for 6 months delivery. |
| Disruption | 10 days at the end Delayed start preferable | 15 days in third week who pays for overtime? |
| Payment | "Shell & Core" priced monthly: pay within 30 days "Fitting out" - 50% on completion       - 50% 2 months later Penalty: 2% per month deducted | Delay penalty: ½% per month "Fitting out": 75% on completion:   25% 1 month later "Fitting out" penalty 1% per month |

He told the Fabriko Team that he believed they were the stronger of the two teams at negotiating – but there would be a balance to be struck because 'Elto need the extension and Fabriko need the work.' He expected that the outcome would depend on the strength and cohesion of the teams.

In the event, Endicott, who had read and absorbed the Italacom case, managed to get agreement to three-quarters of their major needs. Arthur Smart felt that he had lost out when some of his objections were not followed through by his team.

## Checklist for Chapter 6

- ☐ Which of the Team Negotiating principles should the Elto team look at? Team working, negotiating tactics, use of specialists?

- ☐ What is the best way to handle specialists as part of teams? Allow them free rein or brief them thoroughly as to their precise role?

- ☐ Are diversionary tactics in team negotiating fair?

- ☐ How should a Leader cope with such tactics by the other party? Cry foul or set about dealing with them?

- ☐ Should the Elto/Fabriko contract be handled by one man?

# 7

# Summing Up

Recently, the well-known footballer, Rio Ferdinand, was asked why he was delaying signing a new contract with Manchester United. He is said to have remarked, *'Delay is purely part of the negotiating process.'*

This remark possibly sums up the main aspect (not to say, objective) of the book, which is to show that negotiation is a 'process' – and not simply a discrete 'action'. The definitions discussed in Chapter 1(pages 13 and 14) show how difficult it is to pin it down. (Someone once described the process as 'trying to get a grip on jelly.' Others have said they could not define it but would know it when they got involved.) The underlying point must surely be that someone is 'buying' something and someone else has something that they are desperate to 'sell'. If the need and desperation are strong enough, an end-point will be reached. Hence my attempt to provide a framework and some tools to ease the process.

But, you may say, framework and tools are all very well but how do they apply to my problem? The four case studies in the book – Honsang motors, Italacom, the Submersibles and Elto/Fabriko – have been put in to answer that problem. Although in each case, tools, structure and strategy are needed, much of the outcome will result from the make-up of the individuals involved. *(I'm told the same applies to Duplicate Bridge!)*

To take the Honsang Motors case, which is designed to emphasise the importance of preparation, the outcome clearly will depend not on detailed worksheets and calculations, but on the characteristics of the two protagonists. Typically, (and this is a wild generalisation) those

## Summing Up

who are recruited, trained and promoted to being purchasing managers aor procurement executives are very often Analyticals (see pages 48 and 49), whereas successful sales people tend to show the attributes of Expressives (page 51). If we use those two patterns of behaviour as a guide, and the two protagonists realise this early on, the process of movement in negotiation will take place more smoothly. Honsang Motors is a case which can be useed for training purpopses by setting up a negotiation where each side is given only their own information and the trainees negotiate in front of a video camera or camcorder for, say, twenty minutes. When the recording of the negotiation is shown, each trainee can learn where he or she made mistakes or when their actions pushed the whole negotiation forward. See the Checklist for Chapter 2 on page 39 provides a useful list of questions not only for the reader but for trainees watching a video recording of the exercise. *(Many of us see ourselves as Dixon, the confident salesman, rather than Bronowski, the new Purchasing Manager.)*

Chapter 3 attempts to present aspects of behaviour in simple terms – to make it easier for us non-specialists to categorise people through observing their behaviour. During your reading of it, you should try to apply the descriptions of behavioural patterns to colleagues, friends and family – and perhaps discuss your own behavioural patterns to see how they fit. And you could add to the questions at the beginning of Chapter 4 – *'Am I a suitable person to be involved in negotiating – or should I delegate it to someone else?'*

The two cases in Chapter 4 illustrate two other major features of negotiating – what one might call the 'Rio Ferdinand approach' – outrageous demand followed by an incommunicado period. And negotiation around house purchase quite often follows the second point of the Italacom case – namely a series of outrageous demands, to each of which the other party starts to haggle. A final overview demonstrates that the whole edifice of the 'seller' has been undermined by the 'nibbles' of the 'buyer'.

The Submersible Case demonstrates that even when professionals on both sides are well prepared, misunderstandings about the 'characteristics' of each of the protagonists can cause considerable disconnectedness. It also recognises that here are underlying differences in culture which may not be apparent on the surface but which can cause upset. The very fact that Tamaka speaks fluent English may well disguise cultural differences between him and the American. But it is also noteworthy that behavioural patterns (which may have no cultural modifiers) can also give clues to an approach – Tamaka seems to be an Analytical, whereas Walbach is an Expressive.

Finally, in the Chapter on Team Negotiation, I have deliberately tried to combine the points made in earlier chapters about preparation, psychology, structure and strategy and put them into the cauldron of Team Negotiation where leadership and group dynamics also play a role. *(Why not set up a team negotiation on your next Training Day based on Harold Endicott's table on page 120?)*

I suggested in Chapter 1 that both existing and potential negotiators may well need careful training and supervised experience. After you have read this book, I hope you will agree.